Jo

By
Caroline Youde

First Printed in 2010

Caroline Youde
2 Jerviston Gardens
London
SW16 3EL

Published by Caroline Youde

British Library Cataloguing in Publication Data
A record of this book is available from the British Library
ISBN 978-0-9564642-0-0

Printed and bound in Great Britain by Think Ink

This book is dedicated to our family and friends, but especially to the medical team to whom I owe my continued existence; and especially Dr Delyth Rich; she literally saved my life.

To David, Joseph and Jake, I love you.

IUD – IntraUterine Death: *death in utero; failure to detect respiration, heartbeat, or definite movement after birth.*

Stillbirth – *when a foetus which has died in the womb, resides within the mother's body.*

I thought long and hard about writing this book and wondered if it was right to put down on paper, details of a very personal experience; but I finally decided I needed too as part of a never ending healing process.

Much of what I have written is from memory, and for the purposes of filling in any gaps, I have included extracts from my medical file, of which I requested a copy of in 2005.

Many times I have poured over its pages, searching for answers to my questions; but more importantly it is of comfort to me; I have very few tangible items in my possession that represent the existence of our son, my file is one of them.

Sometimes I refer to it so that I can transport myself back in time; not too relive the anguish, but to retrieve old feelings that help me feel close to my boy.

The focus of this book moves between our loss and my recovery. This was not my initial intention, but I decided that to understand the enormity of the whole experience and the impact it has had on our lives, every detail needed to be noted.

I sincerely hope that others who have lost loved ones or those who have had to face traumatic circumstances; may find comfort amongst the pages of this book as our experience was not all bad.

Fundamentally, however, this book has been written to bring life to our son. He was perfect in every way and we love him dearly. The photographs we have are not proudly displayed; they are private and carefully stored. To the world outside we have only one (living) child - it's hard to explain to him why his brother died. I simply say that God was short of an Angel and Joseph was chosen - it's what I believe.

Prelude

David and I had been together 4 years when we married in July 1999. I'm a London girl who had opted to move to South Wales, to settle in my husband's hometown. A move I have never regretted.

Our relationship was similar to many couples and we made the most of our freedom; sailing and camping to name but a few of our favourite hobbies. Our wedding was a wonderful event; filled with many great memories of a perfect day.

So it came as no surprise when, after 18mths of marriage, I started to feel broody. What female doesn't when they have everything? Loving husband, nice home, good job, 2 cars...

We tried for a while, but nothing seemed to be happening. Then, in early February 2001... Bingo! I was pregnant. I couldn't believe it as it had at first seemed like something you just talked about... dreamed about... handing baby over to Dad, phoning numerous relatives and friends... we we're to be parents, it was as simple as that!

Our families of course were thrilled; David's parents especially, as they were to become 1st time grandparents (David's older brother Mark and his wife Camilla elected not to have children).

My own parents, however, were becoming dab hands at the whole thing as my brother Nigel and his wife Trish were about to deliver number 3; but our child was just as important. After all I was their "little girl", so that special bond between Mother and Daughter was to develop to new heights. My own Grandmother, who at the ripe old age of 85 was spending a few weeks in hospital due to an evident deterioration in health, was delighted; for her it was to be great-grandchild number 4, but sadly she passed away soon after we broke the news.

By mid term I was feeling fantastic. I had experienced the pleasures of morning sickness early on as well as incredible bouts of hunger.

I remember one occasion when I had eaten the best part of a loaf for breakfast before heading off to the shops, only to then abandon my plans when I arrived at the supermarket, in favour of MacDonald's!! I had heard of eating for two, but this felt more like twenty-two.

How some women can actually lose weight whilst pregnant is beyond me? I knew then that I was not going to be one of the lucky ones who could claim they had got back into their jeans a week after birth. In fact, I was contemplating ordering myself a nice little two-man tent to wear.

But my erratic food swings soon settled down and by 16 weeks I was glowing and full of energy. My cravings were down to a minimum and David had resided himself to the fact that until our baby was born, he would be eating roast pork, crackling and apple sauce every Sunday (I gave up telling him that Tesco had mysteriously run out of chickens).

I consulted my pregnancy books weekly, just in case I had missed something about my baby's development that I could discuss in work the next day... after all, I was the first woman in history who was about to have a baby (how they put up with me I'll never know).

In what seemed a frighteningly short space of time, my maternity leave start date materialised; Friday 7th September.

Ironically I had to attend hospital for a final scan on the exact same day. Apparently I was carrying excessive fluid and the midwife was finding it difficult to gauge the size of the baby.

Being so late into my pregnancy I wasn't worried and stared at the monitor in amazement as I witnessed our child pursing his lips. How he (I always referred to baby as "he") had grown since my 20-week scan was amazing. He was now so big that the monitor could only show part of his face; I could even make out the Cupid's bow in his top lip.

David unfortunately couldn't leave work to be with me and was therefore missing the event, but at the time it was no big deal. Looking back, it now seems so unfair that he never got to see his son in this way.

*

Having been so careful for so long, I then couldn't believe that on leaving the hospital, I stumbled and fell. Worse of all I fell on the curb stone edge, banging my bump on the corner. Because I was outside the pre-natal clinic, midwives came running from all directions and I was ushered into a room for immediate observations - 20 minutes of worry ticked by.

After monitoring the baby and checking that my waters hadn't broken, I was allowed to leave with a clean bill of health.

Mother and baby were fine; all that excess fluid was certainly doing its job.

Saturday/Sunday, 29th/30th September

Officially this was our last weekend as expectant parents; our baby was due the following week (October 6th). Failing his arrival, I was booked in on the 11th for inducement, but seeing as how I was going to be 32 on the 12th; I was keeping my fingers crossed that baby was going to be on time as I didn't want to be in hospital on my birthday.

Having successfully nagged David into finishing the nursery a few weeks earlier, my time spent at home had been used to prepare everything from making up the cot, to washing and filling the shelves with a multitude of baby grows, socks and mittens.

In short I now had nothing to do. The Moses basket was standing to attention in our bedroom, the pram was all ready to go in the hallway and my blue hospital bag was on standby.

So on the Saturday morning I had my hair cut and went for a pedicure as a last ditch attempt to feel feminine; instead of the beached whale I had become!

I was about to begin a phase of sleepless nights that would result in bags bigger than any suitcase you could ever imagine; plus my social diary was to be replaced with endless days of slopping around in PJ's and slippers.

Make up was to become a thing of the past, at least until I had established a routine, and my hair was purposely kept short to save on blow drying time.

Plenty of women will scoff at what I have just written, and quite rightly so as having a baby is considered quite routine to many, but this was my first time and I was under no illusion that it was going to be anything less than a huge shock to both of us.

Later that afternoon David and I went for a long walk around the lakes, not far from our home. It was hoped by me that a slow amble would allow gravity to take over and kick start my contractions, but alas no, so I resorted to other means such as a hot bath.

I had also heard that riding a bicycle over cobblestones was a tried and tested method; but sense prevailed on this one. Besides, even if I could swing my leg over (!), there were no cobbles that I knew of.

*

On the Sunday I completed my music tape, filled with my favourite songs to help take my mind off the labour. It was an idea suggested by the midwives during antenatal classes.

David and I also tried out the TENS machine that we had rented from Boots.

For those of you unfamiliar with the device, it's a small machine that connects to your lower back via a series of sticky pads and wires. It emits a very low electrical current that tingles and takes the edge of any contractions. You can adjust the strength in accordance with the level of pain you are experiencing.

I for one was all for pain relief. At this stage, my initial birth plan did not include an epidural as I'm not very good with needles; but that was about to change, thanks to a very nice man called Dr Andrew Bagwell, consultant anaesthetist.

Unbeknownst to me, he had been invited to our final antenatal class (which was fast approaching). With his calm approach on the subject and reassuring smile, I was to be convinced that should all else fail; the complete and utter numbing of my lower half was definitely the way forward; I could only hope that labour lasted long enough to fit it all in!

But before all that I was due a visit by my midwife. Home attendance was not normal, especially on a Sunday, however my blood pressure had been a little high during my previous check up and Steph wanted to review the situation.

Of course I was relieved when she said all was ok, but secretly I was a little disappointed; I had hoped she would have me admitted and induced, as by now I was feeling fat and fed up. I guess that sounds a little crazy, but trust me, when you have spent the last nine months sharing your body with another person, you begin to want it back.

When she had gone, we began our video diary. It was David's idea to film me (whom he lovingly referred to as "Sumo"!) and the nursery as a kind of pre-arrival sequence.

It was to be the start of many hours of footage dedicated to our baby's every move. Eventually we would share these moments with him as he grew older.

The camera was a new purchase. Apparently, pregnant women hovering around the audio counter in Comet's are considered to be "a done deal", according to the salesman who served me that is.

I guess it's true as we all tend to view a vast majority of our child's growth through a lens. I know my parents did and we have the cine-film to prove it! (Being of a certain age, cine-cameras preceded camcorders).

As the weekend was drawing to a close, we focused on the week ahead. Tuesday, last day at antenatal and Camilla's birthday; Wednesday was my parents wedding anniversary - cards for both events had already been posted. Thursday was my last scheduled check up with Steph; I couldn't believe that I had reached my 40th week already.

Whilst David and I sat together our conversation turned to news we had recently received concerning a couple we knew; sadly they had experienced a miscarriage at 16 weeks.

We were so sorry for them but at the same time, grateful that our pregnancy had passed without any serious complications.

But life's a bitch; we just didn't know it yet.

Hospital

1

Wednesday 3rd October

I woke at around 7.30am, David was already dressed. It was University day for him as he was studying for an MBA and therefore always headed into work early before evening classes began.

For me it was another day watching Kilroy, surfing the Internet and taking yet another long warm bath. I checked my overnight bag again; did I have all I needed?

As I pottered around the house, I wondered when that first twinge would send a signal to my brain, telling it that operation labour was about to commence. But baby was quiet today - I pushed my concerns to the back of my head.

It was late afternoon and whilst I stood cooking chilli for tea I thought again as to when I had last felt baby move. Normally my warm baths invoked a reaction, but today I had felt nothing.

I sat for a while, convinced that I had simply not noticed; I had grown use to feeling and seeing tiny elbows and feet push and distort my tummy into some of the most bizarre shapes – but by now I was beginning to feel uneasy.

As I didn't want to panic David, I phoned my sister in law; after all she'd had 3 kids and knew much about pregnancy.

She said that as there wasn't much room for baby to manoeuvre, movement becomes difficult and that I should sit quietly for a while to allow even the slightest of flutters register in my head. I explained I had already tried this so her follow up advice was simple, I should phone the hospital.

But phoning the hospital seemed too dramatic... they were busy enough without a paranoid mother-to-be calling, but I did as I was told. The advice I received was short and sweet. I was to report to pre-natal for an immediate check up and stop apologising for bothering them!

But who do I get to drive? I couldn't. I barely fitted behind the wheel and David was too far away; besides I couldn't drag him back for some silly notion, so I decided to call Debs. She and her husband Richard are amongst our closest friends and over the past months, had shared in our joy.

By now it was early evening, but she didn't mind. During the short drive to the hospital, I remember clutching my medical file and saying how stupid I felt. It had only been 24hrs since I had attended hospital for my final antenatal class where everyone had wished me well (I was furthest along in my pregnancy). I was convinced that before I even set foot on the ward, baby would spring into action and start tap dancing around my lower abdomen.

On arrival everyone was very kind. I was shown into an examination room and told to lie on the bed. A midwife appeared with an ear trumpet. I thought that more modern and up to date instruments had superseded such devices; but on reflection I wonder if this method allowed the midwife to prepare herself for the worst, before having to break any potential bad news to expectant parents.

I knew where the heartbeat was as I had heard it so often when attending my weekly checkups; but why was it taking so long for her to find it? The ear trumpet was substituted for a sonographer, an electronic hand held device used for listening to the baby's heartbeat. It has a speaker attached so that you too can listen to your baby's heart pounding away, as well as the various gurgling sounds of the fluids surrounding your most precious of bundles.

As soon as she placed the sensor on my abdomen I knew something was wrong. It was too quiet. Not a sound.

As she moved it around trying to detect a heartbeat I started to feel very hot, my heart began to beat faster, my breathing became shallow. Debs left her chair and walked over; she began to rub my foot as a means to comfort me. A second midwife joined us and knowing glances were exchanged.

Within what seemed like seconds, a young female doctor entered the room and a portable scanner was brought in. A piece of me was clinging onto the hope that this wonder of modern technology was to contradict my inner most frantic feelings; but it's a pity that technology isn't so obliging. Within minutes my worst nightmare had become a reality. No heartbeat could be detected. My baby was dead.

As I sit here now, writing this, words could never describe how I felt...

I don't remember how I ended up sitting in a private room, staring at a wall, but that's where I found myself. My chair was beside a bed, with a window to my right and the door to my left. Debs was there; I said to call David but not to tell him. Try and sound normal, just say that I was having a check up and could he come. She left the room to make one of the hardest phone calls ever.

I was calm and composed but emotionally I was totally disconnected. I had been told my baby was dead, so that was that. Nothing I could do. In fact it was all becoming clear. People had to be told, parents, friends; in my head I began to prioritise whom. It was as though I was in a parallel world, one where my life was now taking a path I could not have envisaged; but this wasn't science fiction, it was real and it was happening to me. Looking back I guess I was in shock.

Debs returned with Richard by her side. She must have been gone a while, but I had no sense of time. I just sat, staring at the wall. Richard stood to my right; Debs sat to my left, holding my hand. No one spoke. It all seemed so surreal. How could this be happening; I had 3 days to go until my official due date; it was all a mistake.

The door opened and David walked in. It was then I broke down and cried. It had suddenly hit me like a thunderbolt that all his hopes and dreams had been shattered and I was responsible. After all it was I who had been charged with looking after this baby, no one else.

As soon as he saw me he knew what had happened. During his drive to the hospital he had called a work colleague who had just had a baby - he was desperate for suggestions as to why his heavily pregnant wife had sent a message that he was to come right away. But what could they say except not to worry and that it was probably all routine.

Richard and Debs left us alone. David held me in his arms and immediately told me how much he loved me. He was very controlled.

Soon after the door opened and we were asked to return to the scanning room; there goes that flicker of hope again! I can only surmise that it was policy for the hospital to be sure that there was nothing they could do and although the doctor had changed, the news was the same, no heartbeat could be detected.

We returned to the private room where we were left to collect our thoughts. It was then that we decided to begin the difficult task of informing our families. I used my mobile phone to call Nigel as my parents had been at his house celebrating their anniversary.

He didn't know what to say except that mum and dad were on their way home, so I rang mum's mobile; they were still driving. I remember asking her to get Dad to pull over, but she knew instantly something was wrong so I just told her.

I can't recall what was said except that I would ring later as we had yet to ring David's parents and brother. But Mark and Camilla were out so we left a message for them to get in touch. We didn't go into detail.

The door opened and again we were called as doctor number three (more senior) had arrived; and so it was that we went through the whole routine for the final time, except during this exam, we were dealt another blow. I was told that I was to deliver naturally; i.e. full labour. I felt sick. David asked about a caesarean but the answer was no. An operation of that sort without the need, medically, was considered too risky. It was a full and intrusive procedure and although tragic, my situation did not warrant it. Those weren't the exact words used, but that's how it felt, harsh and totally unfair.

Before the scanner was switched off, I asked a question, "What sex was the baby?" – It was a boy, my instincts had been correct.

We returned to our room accompanied by doctor number two. I remember him as being so kind and gentle who spoke softly and with empathy. He backed the decision for a natural delivery but reassured me that I would be given every drug possible to ease the pain. By the time he finished I was accepting of the situation.

We discussed what was to happen - David and I were to go home to get some sleep and return the next morning when I would be induced. We could of course wait until my body naturally went into labour but I wanted the ordeal over with as quickly as possible so opted to return first thing.

As we left via the maternity entrance we passed a couple that were leaving with their newborn baby; I suddenly broke down and fell to my knees crying. I didn't care about the stares I attracted as David helped me up and supported me to the car. We drove to Richard and Deb's house. It was now around 9:30pm.

As soon as David walked in he finally let go of his emotions and the tears came. Richard was shaking his head in disbelief. No one really spoke except to ask if we'd like a brandy. I politely refused, as I never did like the taste, so instead I opted for a sherry!

By now I had composed myself and in time it would become apparent that when I faltered, David was the stronger, but when it was his turn to crumble, I would suddenly gain control. It was a subconscious arrangement that would get us through the events to come.

When we did finally go home, the house felt empty. Silly really as it had always just been David and I, but somehow the life that had been inside me had already started to make an impact and even though we hadn't actually seen nor held our child, his presence could be felt in the house as we had gone about our day to day routine.

The phone rang at around 10:45pm; it was Mark. He knew what had happened as he had rung his mum when he couldn't get an answer from our phone (we had been driving home when he first called).

David answered but couldn't speak. I remember standing in the kitchen holding the phone in one hand whilst hugging David with my other arm.

The conversation was short but to the point. Offers of support were given, I said thank you and hung up. By now we were both drained and needed to get some sleep; but it felt almost impossible.

At first we just lay there in silence, and then David started to sob quietly until he eventually succumbed to the sheer exhaustion of the whole event. I too must have drifted off as I woke later at around 4:30am; and although early, we decided to prepare for the hospital.

David rang ahead to advise them we were on our way. I was upstairs getting dressed when suddenly my waters broke. This threw me into a state of confusion as my head was telling me this must be my body starting to "reject" the dead baby inside me, but at the same time my heart was breaking as I wondered if my labour had simply begun 1 day too late, and had this happened yesterday, would my baby be alive today?

With a heavy heart we left the house.

2

Thursday 4th October

Walking through the doors of the maternity department was very hard and already we looked dejected and beaten.

Almost immediately I was faced with a new mum carrying her baby, but the numbness I had felt was back, and I didn't bat an eyelid as we were led past into a private room (ironically the same one as the night before).

Over the next few hours various doctors and midwives came and went, offering tea & toast, taking bloods etc, and it wasn't until 9:30am that I finally saw a familiar face when Steph arrived. Without a word she walked over and hugged me. When she drew back I could see the tears in her eyes. Her first words were "I'm so sorry", to which I replied it wasn't her fault and that it was ok. It somehow made me feel better that I was comforting her, even though that was not what she was looking for. We chatted for a while before she had to leave.

I had been told that I would be taken down at around midday and in what seemed like no time at all I found myself walking a long corridor to a delivery suite situated the furthest away; all around me I could hear women groaning and babies crying.

The room was large and had a telly. I changed into my nightdress and lay on the bed. David drew up a chair alongside me. Shortly afterwards we were joined by a midwife, an anaesthetist and 2 assistant nurses.

The epidural procedure was explained, and whilst an intravenous drip was inserted into the back of my left hand, David stood as I turned to sit sideways on the bed.

One of the nurses spoke to break the tension in the room, except instead of words of comfort she jokingly asked if we were thinking about trying for another or if one was enough?

At first we didn't know what to say and I asked myself if she in fact knew what had happened; David hesitated a little then gently said that we would give it another go.

The realisation of what she had said suddenly dawned on her and we watched as the colour drained from her face; she had known but for that split second, had gone into auto drive, letting her usual patter override her thought process.

I felt sorry for her as she apologised profusely but in reality it remains one of those key moments that David or I have never forgotten.

The anaesthetist was ready to begin and although not painful, I found the procedure very uncomfortable.

I remember crying saying that all this discomfort was for nothing, but soon it was over and I settled back to let the drug do its job. At around 1:30pm I was administered a pessory to encourage labour.

And so we began the process that I had been waiting for, except it was not how I had planned over and over in my head. When I felt the first twinge I would call David, he in turn would call the hospital - and then, basing my conclusions on my own mother's experience, I would be in labour for about 7 hours.

David would be the first to hold the baby, before rushing off to phone everyone. After a day or so we would return home. When it was time for me to return to work, baby would go to nursery and, as I wanted to breastfeed, I would invest in a breast pump. Simple!

Anyway, back to reality....

The next few hours were uneventful. I was monitored for signs of labour and although I couldn't feel anything, I was told my contractions had started.

As I drifted in and out of sleep, I was aware of the TV being on. Now and again David would put his head on the bed to grab a quick 5 minutes shuteye.

Over the course of the afternoon, we had 3 midwife changes and at each change we were asked the same question, "how did we want baby presented to us?" Each time we gave the same answer - once born, we wanted him cleaned and wrapped, placed in my arms, then left alone to be with our son.

We couldn't think any more ahead than that and hadn't even considered what would happen afterwards until we were asked about an autopsy; quite calmly we replied that we wanted to know what had happened, for future planning purposes, and therefore verbally consented.

Now apparently due to historic events concerning the retention of babies' organs by another hospital, there was paperwork for us to sign but it never materialised.

Although noted in my medical file as an oversight (it was felt by the midwife to be an inappropriate time to present us with such forms), we see it as a blessing that there was nothing to support our decision; but I'll come to that later.

As with all bereavements, there was also a counsellor on standby and although I'm sure she would have been very sympathetic and kind, she was a stranger who had no idea who we were. All we needed were our family and friends, people who understood us and made us feel safe.

By 4:30pm I was fully dilated. Mine was proving to be a rapid labour and although I felt ready to push, I was encouraged to hold on.

I began to feel some considerable discomfort. Not a sharp pain or a stomach cramp, but an incredible pressure lower down as if my bottom was about to explode - it's the only way I can describe it! David called for assistance and my epidural was topped up.

Soon it was time for me to start pushing and it was at this point that Dr Delyth Rich joined us. She introduced herself as being the Registrar on call and would help me deliver our baby. With much encouragement from David, Delyth and Clare (midwife), I began the final stage.

Over the next hour or so I pushed, groaned, grunted and pushed. David was amazing as he continued to support me, even though deep down he was finding it hard to watch me trying so desperately to deliver our son; both knowing that it was all in vain.

Little by little baby began to descend but it wasn't long before I became exhausted and would have to undergo an assisted delivery using forceps; in preparation an episiotomy was performed (a small cut to assist a vaginal delivery).

With one final push the head was out. I remember Delyth commenting on how big baby was and how his shoulders were proving difficult to extract, but soon it was over and our son, Joseph Michael Youde, was born at 9:20pm, weighing a whopping 8lb 6oz.

Immediately afterwards I was given an injection in the left thigh to speed the delivery of the placenta; it's quite a normal procedure.

Everything was quiet. Joseph had at first been taken by Clare to prepare him as agreed; and I could at last close my eyes and take stock of what had just happened.

I was so tired that I drifted off to sleep and it was only when I felt a huge pressure in my left hand did I begin wake; when I opened my eyes there were a number of "white coats" standing where David had been sitting only moments before.

But where was David? And why did my hand hurt so much? As my eyes focused I recognised Dr Andrew Bagwell (how ironic); he was squeezing a bag of fluid in through my drip. Delyth was at the foot of the bed, pushing down on my abdomen.

I didn't know what was happening, I just wanted to sleep but there was talk about taking me to theatre; then the bed started to move.

David appeared by my side looking pale. As I looked up at him I told him to call Richard, as I didn't want him to be left alone; it was as if my mind suddenly cleared and I knew instinctively what had to be done.

Remember how I said that subconsciously we seemed to take it in turns to be strong? Now it was my turn again, even if just for one brief moment.

Then David was gone and I became disorientated as ceiling lights passed overhead (just like an episode of Holby City) and people were stepping back, hugging the walls as I was rushed past; but the thing I remember most was Delyth; she was still seated at the base of the bed "kneading" my abdomen.

Within moments we were passing through the doors into theatre. I so wanted to sleep but Andrew kept saying, "stay with me, stay with me".

I was lifted onto the table and became aware of someone tapping the back of my right hand (apparently in an effort to find a vein, which by now were collapsing).

Andrew wanted me to drink something but I just coughed it up. I felt rushed, the atmosphere was frantic.

An oxygen mask was placed over my nose and mouth and I was told to breathe deep and close my eyes. At last I was being allowed to slip out of consciousness and sleep; convincing myself that in what would feel like moments, I would wake and it would all be over.

To the words "we'll have to open her tummy up", I drifted off.

Since my experience, people have assumed that I wouldn't remember any of my time in theatre. Of course there are elements I have no memory of as I was under the anaesthetic, but until then, I can recall every moment as if it were happening now.

I can feel the tension that was present in the room as well as the physical sensations that resulted from the medical team attending to me.

I knew I was dying; it's something I will never forget, and even though I knew, I wasn't scared. I felt exhausted but peaceful; and if allowed I would have quite happily surrendered.

My mum once hailed it as a miracle that I survived. But I'm not the miracle; the medical team who fought against all the odds are. My body was ready to give up; they simply would not allow that to happen.

Extract from medical notes: Midwife Clare Swallow:

22:06: Dr Rich requests IV augmentin (antibiotic) *which I went to get. On return anaesthetic team were present – Dr Bagwell.*

22:10: I litre of haes given (contains platelets for clotting process)

22:17: Miss A Rees phoned and on her way (consultant)

22:20: Another litre of haes given and preparation made for transfer to theatre. Blood and FFP sent for (FFP, fresh frozen plasma. The fluid component of blood lacking the cells but containing all the necessary plasma proteins used to restore the protein clotting factors)

22:30: Into theatre. Blood transfusion commenced. Miss Rees and Dr Appadurai present (consultant anaesthetist)

22:50: Miss Rees asking for another consultant to help – A Fiander, Mr Roberts, J Evans & Mr Beattie contacted not all have replied yet.

23:05: RM J Holden has spoken to dad regarding baby – he doesn't want to make any decisions without first speaking to Caroline.

23:20: A Fiander arrives (specialist in foetal medicine).

P Clyburn in attendance (consultant anaesthetist)

23:25: Mr Beattie arrives (senior consultant from The Heath University Hospital; courtesy of an emergency ambulance)

23:30: Mr Roberts arrived (senior consultant)

23:30: Knife to skin.

23:55: Attempts being made to repair uterus. Dr Rich and myself speak to family again to update them.

00:15: Decision made to perform hysterectomy. Partner informed and also told that Caroline will be going into ICU for probably a couple of days. He appears to understand. I have offered to find him accommodation within hospital.

01:10: Operation completed. Total fluids given in theatre 46.5 units: Blood 23 units, FFP 6 units, Cryo 14 units & Haes 3.5 units

01:15: Suturing commenced.

01:45: Suturing completed.

* * *

Extract from medical notes: Miss Alex Rees:

Called at 22:15 to patient bleeding. Arrived to find patient in theatre, anaesthetised with major haemorrhage and DIC*.

Still bleeding. Help summoned. Decision to perform laparotomy (incision through the abdominal wall) - *ruptured uterus confirmed.*

*Disseminated intravascular coagulation (DIC) is the activation of blood clotting mechanisms and leads to the formation of small blood clots inside the blood vessels throughout the body. It is common in the critically ill, and may participate in the development of multiple organ failure. The only effective treatment is the reversal of the underlying cause. Platelets may be transfused if massive hemorrhage is occurring. The prognosis for those with DIC, regardless of cause, is often grim, leading the initials to be known colloquially as "death is coming".

When the job was complete I was to be transferred to intensive care; my breathing was supported by a ventilator, a drain was in-situ via my abdomen to collect the blood that continued to seep from the wound and a urine catheter bag inserted.

My operation sheet reported five surgeons were in attendance: A Rees/A Roberts/A Fiander/B Beattie/D Rich; and three anesthetists: P Clyburn/A Bagwell/I Appadurai; along with two nurses: K Husband/J Holden. But praise must also be given to the orderlies on duty that night (I do not know their names). They were there to receive the abundance of fluids, which were delivered by ambulance under police escort; and who continued to work vigorously, fetching and carrying anything that was required by the team. And the labs teams, on hand 24/7 to check and cross check bloods.

3

Friday 5th October

As I opened my eyes I was drawn to a window on my left. The sky was blue. I felt very groggy and had to blink hard several times before my eyelids would stay open - I could hear someone saying, "She's waking up".

With my vision clearing, I could see David standing by my side, on my right. Richard and Debs stood behind him. Delyth was to my left, near the foot of my bed. Although smiling, there were tears in their eyes.

I couldn't talk and for some reason thought I had had a tracheotomy; I guess it was because I remembered someone pressing on my throat as the anaesthetic had taken hold, but it was the tube from my ventilator restricting my vocal cords. I felt calm and rested. There was no pain.

According to my notes, it was 8am, and the feeling of serenity I was experiencing during that 1st awakening was far removed from the drama that had taken place only an hour earlier when at 7am David had been called from his bed (the hospital had found him a vacant room so that he could stay for the remainder of the night).

I was showing signs of increased blood loss in my drain as well as an increase in abdominal distension (swelling). It was believed that I had again begun to haemorrhage.

Alex Rees had arrived back at 730am. She noted that all observations (pulse, blood pressure etc) were stable, but I was to be transferred immediately to theatre if there was a sudden deterioration.

The news that I was showing signs of a relapse only added to the living nightmare that David could not wake up from, and he collapsed to his knees and cried – a call was made to Richard and Debs asking if they could return; it was understood that David needed support.

Having only just made it to her bed, Delyth had also been telephoned; she immediately returned to the hospital. She spoke encouragingly to David and suggested that he should just talk to me.

Now this may sound like something out of a fairy tale, stuffed full of romanticisms, but at the sound of his voice, I started to wake. Simple as that; it's no wonder there wasn't a dry eye in the house!

I don't know if you'd call it self-preservation, but once I was conscious, I seemed to quickly want to wake up and by 9:25am it was noted, *"Obs stable, much more alert. Abdomen not distending any further"*.

It was as if my brain was now telling my body it had a job to do and that job was to get better fast. When I think about it, I guess it was my way of feeling that I had some control back and very soon I was communicating using a pen and paper (I still have my scribbles). I asked where I was. Was I in tact? Where was Joseph? Did Mum and Dad know?

I was told I was in intensive care, recovering from emergency surgery. My in-laws, Mike and Wendy, were waiting to see me and did I feel up to it? "Yes", I wrote. I wanted to see them, to show them I was ok.

Mum and Dad were also on their way, as was my brother and sister in-law; David had rung them shortly after I was taken into theatre. He said there had been complications following Joseph's birth but that I was ok.

There was no sense in alarming them as they had a long drive from London, plus he wanted them to get some sleep.

They had no idea how serious the situation was, which is why when it was thought my condition was deteriorating, it was suggested by Richard that they should be diverted to Mike and Wendy's house in case the worst happened.

It was felt that any bad news should be broken to them before they reached the hospital, and so in light of their imminent arrival, Mike and Wendy soon returned home; except now they could greet my family with the good news that I was awake and the prognosis more positive.

Shortly afterwards, everyone left leaving David and I alone, only the staff on duty remained.

My ventilator was removed, quickly and painlessly. I was breathing unaided but had to wear an oxygen mask at all times.

I felt parched, but I was "nil by mouth", which meant I could only have the inside of my mouth swabbed using a large, cotton bud soaked in water (throughout the day and when I thought no one would notice, I would suck as much water off the swab as I could. I felt like a naughty child, secretly sipping champagne at a wedding when the adults weren't looking).

To ensure that fluid was not collecting in my lungs due to my lack of mobility, a very nice lady from the Physio department arrived to assess my ability to cough. I had to try to clear my throat which proved more difficult than it sounds; my body simply would not co-operate so I had to force myself to cough – which hurt allot!

If you take a moment to acknowledge which muscles you use to cough, you'll notice your abdomen tenses to assist your diaphragm. Even with the morphine the pain was very unpleasant.

As I had to do this exercise regularly, a towel was placed across my tummy and I was shown how I could use it by pulling it gently down to try and minimise the movement, thus minimise the pain – it helped, but it still hurt.

However there was an incentive. If I could not shift the fluid myself I would have to have a tube inserted to drain away the mucus.

Needless to say I put in 100% effort to get it right.

Alex returned at 11:30am and a curtain was pulled around the bed; David took my hand - funnily enough I could sense bad news was coming!

She started to explain that I had been very sick; I had suffered a catastrophic haemorrhage and had to be taken into theatre to establish what was going on. She said it had been necessary to open my abdomen.

But before she could say anymore I just came out with it, "I've had a hysterectomy, haven't I?" David squeezed my hand and at the same time put his head down on the bed.

Alex was taken aback and wanted to know how I knew, but that's just it - I just "knew".

Even to this day I can't explain it and can only conclude that my brain had pieced it all together. Whether it was because my mum had had one, coupled with the memory of Delyth kneading my tummy; I don't know – call it woman's intuition if you like.

I turned to David and said I was ok, he looked so sad; Alex continued.

I had had a blood transfusion during surgery and was currently on morphine. Since my arrival in ICU I had been given a further one unit of blood. I was hooked up by various wires to a multitude of monitors, all of which were out of sight as they were behind my bed; and a number of drips had been inserted into both arms.

Stats would continue to be taken every half hour to monitor changes in blood pressure and temperature; just in case they had to react quickly to a possible down turn in my recovery. Fluid levels in my blood drain would be constantly measured, as well as my girth size to ascertain any increases in abdominal distension.

With regards to my kidney functions, during surgery my body had begun shutting down vital organs in an effort to preserve the brain and I had gone into renal failure; until I woke up and began passing urine, it was not known if my kidneys had indeed failed; but Alex was happy that they seemed to be functioning ok.

A CVC line, or central venous catheter, had been inserted into my neck, just under my left ear, and was being used to administer medication as well as obtain cardiovascular measurements (in brief, it is a small tube that passes through the body via the jugular vein and resides in the right atrium of the heart; it is held in place on the neck by a small stitch).

It was a lot to take in. We sat for a moment in silence before Alex left. Dave and I just looked at each other but before I could say anything we were joined by an ICU nurse who was to give me a bed bath.

Now as anyone who has been in hospital knows, when you're feeling as though you've gone 10 rounds with Mike Tyson, you don't care what you look like or what parts of your anatomy are exposed!

As she worked wonders with her sponge and towel, the nurse remarked that it was always best to remove the dried blood from the face and body when one is about to receive visitors (my family had arrived).

I remember thinking, what blood? Holby City patients were never covered in blood, in fact when they awoke from major surgery their hair and makeup was still in place!

But that thought was soon extinguished when I was gently rolled onto my side; my abdomen exploded with pain, every movement was agony and it didn't seem to matter that I was on morphine.

When she had finished, I felt exhausted. I had just about enough energy to brush my teeth (no swallowing allowed!) and comb my hair (that too was matted with blood).

David asked if I was up to seeing my family – I was but there was to be one condition: no tears; I didn't want people to start blubbering all over me; I couldn't handle that. The fact of the matter was I was awake and feeling positive.

When she was told this, Mum replied, "That sounds like Caroline!"

And so I saw my parents for the first time since they had last visited us in the July, when they had arrived with gifts from family and friends; Mum had been so proud of the cardigans she had knitted.

I was in the right hospital, just the wrong ward. Instead of postnatal, I was in ICU. Instead of having a crib by my bed, I was surrounded by machines.

But they were still smiling, though it was more out of relief than joy.

They chatted away; I can't really remember what was said. Mum took up the job of administering the mouth swab; only this time she would tell me off for sucking (that's typical of my Mother, she doesn't miss a trick – it was the same when my brother started smoking at school!).

Speaking of Nigel, he too was waiting to see me (only two visitors at a time allowed).

Again I can't recall the conversation but what I do remember though was feeling a sense of relief that my family hadn't seen me when I was on the ventilator; I don't think they would have coped as well. Especially my Dad; I had noticed the shimmer of a tear in his eye but he did well to try and hide it.

In ICU people aren't allowed to stay for long, as the staff know how easily you tire, and out of concern for my well being, my visits were put on hold for the rest of the day; except of course for David.

However he had opted to go home for a while, he too needed to rest but promised he would be back later. As I was feeling stronger I was happy for him to go, besides, I was to be allowed an ice cube to suck on later that afternoon, so I had something to look forward to!

With everyone gone I watched the staff go about their duties. When it was my turn to have my stats read I would ask if everything was ok; knowing became a kind of comfort blanket.

It was late afternoon when I was visited by a gentleman called Mr Adrian Roberts. I knew the name as it had been printed at the bottom of all my pre-natal appointment letters and test results when I was pregnant, but we had never met.

As he introduced himself I remember thinking how he had missed all the drama. I had no idea that he had been one of the consultants called to assist Alex in theatre. Nor did I realise how fundamental to my continued well being this highly respected, softly spoken man was to become in the years that followed.

For now, he was simply another part of the team that would provide guidance with regards to my recovery plan. He checked my notes, wrote a few lines and left.

By early evening David was back. Whilst the world busied itself around us, we held hands. Because of the oxygen mask anything I said sounded muffled so I was just happy to lie in bed as David read the paper he had brought.

Doctors came and went, not just to see me, but also other patients that shared the ward. Thinking back it seemed as though I was the only one, but there were another 5 beds, all occupied; hidden away behind their own curtain. Everything was always so quiet.

As the day had progressed, so had my inner strength. Mentally I felt on top of the world. All thoughts of how I had come to be there had been pushed, subconsciously, to the back of my mind. My focus was purely on myself and my fight to get better.

Does that sound selfish? Probably.

*

Late into the evening a Doctor was called to observe the amount of blood that had collected in my drain.

Although the staff did a very good job of hiding it, concern was rising; for a second time in less than 24hrs and a return to theatre was being considered.

David was quietly informed but I was completely oblivious to what was going on, so didn't think anything of it when Richard re-appeared. I just thought he'd come to visit, I hadn't noticed David slip out for a brief moment to call him.

Internally David felt sick as his anxiety levels had begun to rise, but he was calm on the outside as he ever so gently, told me what was happening.

I felt scared, I didn't want to return to theatre but David said it would be ok as this time everything would be more controlled; but my fear was based on the additional pain I would experience - it never crossed my mind that they may not be able to stop the bleeding.

Thankfully the crisis soon subsided after further checks were carried out. The Doctor on call concluded that the blood collected was a reasonable amount for one day and believed that the flow had in fact slowed down. To be absolutely sure, new readings were taken and fresh observations made. Within half an hour it was confirmed that the flow was on the decline.

Everyone breathed a sigh of relief, but for David it was the final straw and he admitted to me that he was physically and mentally exhausted. I told him to go home for the night and sleep.

I think it's important to remember that David had just lost his son and almost his wife; he needed to take a step back to allow himself time to adjust to what had transpired over the past 24 hours.

In my eyes I had the easiest job of all; I wasn't going anywhere. All I had to do was lie in bed and rest whilst nurses attended to my every need. There was always something happening that kept me distracted from past events whilst David had to return to an empty house, surrounded by baby monitors, clothes, toys... he had to face our loss all on his own.

*

Just before midnight two young, female doctors appeared on the ward. They moved from bed to bed, reviewing everyone's notes. Eventually they came to me. I felt like an exhibit on show. What were they discussing between themselves in hushed whispers? I was scared, as I didn't know who they were. Was I ok? Was something wrong?

Then as quickly as they appeared they left. In time I was to learn they had in fact been students - let's hope that someone has since taught them the importance of introducing oneself to patients, not only to elay their fears, but because it's common courtesy!

Diane was an ICU nurse; she came to sit by me. I remember her as being very solemn and what she told me only impacted on the knowledge I had gained from Alex Rees.

Diane remarked how well I was doing and was amazed that I was even awake. She told me she had been on duty the night I had been admitted, and how poorly I was. She did not think then that my chances were very good and could not believe that less than 24 hours later, I was awake and talking (and as anyone who knows me will confirm, talking is very much my strong point.)

When faced once more with the enormity of the situation, I again felt disbelief that I had been (was) so ill.

I was like a sponge eager to absorb as much information as I could about what had happened, and as you'll come to learn, my quest did not end when I eventually left hospital; in fact it has never ended and I am constantly researching on the internet and re-reading my medical notes for snippets of new information to help me digest exactly what happened. This may seem to some that by not letting go of the past, I am stopping myself from moving on; but for me, keeping these memories alive keeps Joseph alive.

I never want to forget what I felt back then as long as I live. Sometimes I lie in bed at night and let my mind wonder back - to feel close to the experience, is to feel close to my son.

Now on the wall across from my bed was a clock that was to become my new best friend.

As I mentioned before I was to be allowed an ice cube to suck on, which was heaven on earth as I was desperately thirsty; so you can imagine my joy when I was told I could have one cube per hour.

The staff were so nice and as they didn't have an ice machine on the ward but knew where one was located, a space was made in the medicine fridge to store some cubes for me!

And so it began that on the hour, every hour, one cube was placed in a plastic cup and left on a chair by my bed. Even if it arrived early, I waited until it was the top of the hour before savouring the taste and sensation of ice-cold water, slowing dissolving on my tongue.

That simple routine got me through my first night - as I watched the minutes turn to hours and as the hours passed, the night slowing ticked by. Staff came and went (I was still on half hourly checks) and once in a while I would be told off for forgetting to replace my oxygen mask after ice cubes.

I did try to sleep but it proved impossible as apart from the half hourly checks, an old lady 3 beds down was gravely ill and her family were arriving, one by one to say their goodbyes - she died in the early hours of the morning. It was terribly sad. But that wasn't the main reason for my lack of sleep; I was experiencing vivid flashbacks every time I closed my eyes; once again I could hear the voices in my head from the night before - frantic calls for assistance and other indistinguishable sounds that would become forever stored within my memory.

4

Saturday 6th October

Today was my official due date; according to the medical team I was doing brilliantly and allowed to eat a yogurt. I only managed a few spoonfuls but it was a start.

David arrived and his spirits were lifted by my progress, which in turn filled me with encouragement. We were both at the beginning of a long road, and without David's strength to draw from, I would not be doing so well – he was (is) my rock.

When I think how I was safely removed from the realities he was facing at home, it fills me with such admiration for the way he coped.

Neighbours and friends who knew nothing of what had happened and thought that my absence was a symbol of good news – would approach him with expectant smiles and enquire as to whether it was a boy or a girl; David would, ever so gently, have to break the news to them.

To put into words our loss, hit him hard. There was nowhere for him to hide.

I, on the other hand, was nicely tucked up in hospital and in some bizarre way, saw it all as some big adventure. I was totally engrossed by the whole situation. I was learning lots of interesting things like how a PCA (patient controlled analgesic) worked. Apparently, every time I pressed the button, a shot of morphine was released, but to prevent overdosing, there was a 5-minute delay.

Also, I was on a waterbed, which was certainly a first for me. (To admit that I felt like this leaves me feeling somewhat uncomfortable but it is the truth; and unless I have an acute case of attention deficiency; I can only surmise that all these distractions helped delay my grieving process and in turn, stay strong).

By mid afternoon I was deemed well enough to be transferred out of ICU and onto the gynaecology ward, "Delyth Ward" (quite a coincidence that the name "Delyth" was to feature so predominantly in my life).

This was a huge relief to me as I had decided that every piece of equipment they unhooked and every change made to relax the stringent checks I had been placed under, was a sign that I was one step closer to being "out of the woods".

David was also relieved at the choice of wards as at first it had been suggested I would be transferred to maternity and into "postnatal"; however this was changed after he made it quite clear that there was no way on earth I was to be placed within a hundred feet of a new born baby, no matter how private the room was.

But I ask you to forget for now about the effect this would have had on me and give some thought to how awful it would have been for anyone visiting me.

If you consider that many hospitals have tight security around babies, and at our unit, visitors have to wait to be "buzzed in" through a security door; can you imagine how David or my/his family would have felt whist waiting to gain entry, standing next to some deliriously happy new dad, carrying a cacophony of flowers and balloons, daubed with the words "its a boy!"

No thanks! Babies were strictly off limits. If the midwives had to continue caring for me (as technically I had still had a baby), then they had to leave their domain and travel the 200 meters or so along the adjoining corridor to the next ward.

*

My arrival into "Delyth" was naturally uneventful, except that I had to give up my waterbed. Hospital beds are ok, but I found I had to have a pillow under my knees to help bend my legs and thus relieve the pull on my abdomen, as well as requiring a multitude of pillows to support my back and head as I couldn't straighten out. I had to lie as if "scrunched up" to feel at all comfortable. I still had my blood drain, urine catheter, central venous line and PCA, but I was down to two drips. My heart monitor and other such electrical devices had also been removed when I left ICU.

The ward staff were equally as lovely and although under midwife care, they carried out the majority of stats that were now being taken every hour as opposed to half hourly. I also swapped my oxygen mask for a small oxygen tube that clipped gently to the base of my nose. When switched on, a bottle producing the oxygen would bubble with water, on the wall just behind my head.

It sounded like a garden water feature and was strangely relaxing.

By early evening I was feeling hungry for MacDonald's of all things, so David popped out to pick up a burger and chips, but I could only manage three small bites. As quickly as it had begun, my appetite was gone and by now the only thing I craved was water.

Whether it was due to being deprived of it during my first 24 hours or because every drop I drank seemed to pass straight from me into my catheter, I couldn't tell, but I drank it by the jug load. The nurses always joked that I could have weed for Britain as they had to frequently change the bag!

Richard came to see how we were both doing and pulled up a chair alongside David. My room was private and surprising cosy. It was October and therefore dark by early evening.

I love this time of year; summer has passed, the autumn leaves are falling and Christmas is coming. It's a time when you light log fires and snuggle up to a good film on the telly.

As I'm not a fan of bright lights, I had only my nightlight on (used by the nurses when they come to check on you). A soft glow filled the room. It all felt very relaxed and calm, so I ventured to ask both Richard and David, what exactly had happened 2 nights ago. In monotone voices they shared with me their experience.

David first:

Joseph had just been born. David was holding my hand; Delyth had begun to suture my episiotomy. During the procedure, my pulse was checked and it was then that all hell broke loose as they couldn't get a reading. An emergency crash team was called and David found himself being pushed back against the wall as the room quickly filled.

A decision was made that I was to be taken to theatre, and as suddenly as it had begun, I was whisked away. David was left standing in the room, alone, with a pool of blood on the floor that trailed off down the corridor. He didn't know how long he stood there for or when he made the call to Richard and Debs, but after what seemed like forever; he walked out of the delivery room to some chairs just outside the door. There he sat patiently waiting; watching as a cleaner cleared up the mess.

Eventually a midwife accompanied him to the relative's waiting room. Questions were asked by her about Joseph, but David wanted to discuss matters with me first. It was then that Richard and Debs joined him.

*

I watched intently as David sat back in his chair and stared at the floor, unable to talk anymore. Richard took up the story:

A team of top consultants were on route to ascertain what was going on and fix the problem. As time ticked by waiting for news, 10 minutes turned into 20; 20 into 40 and so on. In fact David and Richard had enough time to drive to a garage and buy a pack of cigarettes and smoke one (even though neither had smoked for years) before Delyth and Clare provided them with news around midnight; I was haemorrhaging and efforts were underway to make good by repair – it was a brief update as they needed to return to theatre.

However, it wasn't long before Delyth returned, this time accompanied by one of the consultants (Mr Roberts).

When they entered the room they asked David to sit down (he later admitted to me that his legs buckled beneath him as he prepared himself for the worst); but David was in such a distressed state that it didn't even register with him what they had to say and Richard found himself having to handle the situation.

It was advised that for now they had managed to stem the bleeding by clamping off a main artery. Efforts had been made to repair what now transpired to be a severely torn uterus, but as the uterus is a muscle, mine would not contract back because it was saturated with blood; the only alternative was to perform a hysterectomy and remove it all together.

David did not speak, but sat with his head in his hands. Richard clarified matters; if they did not remove it, then I would die, therefore they had no choice but to proceed.

Mr Roberts of course agreed (as absurd as it sounds, they had to seek permission). Delyth said they would be back in a short while to update everyone on my progress, but another hour and a half was yet to pass and David was to remain in a constant state of turmoil.

*

Debs told me years later that David was almost motionless during the whole time he waited for that final update and spoke only once. He said that we had come to hospital to have a baby; that was all. The events that had taken place had completely overwhelmed him, and for an experienced ex-forces man, he was very much in shock.

*

Delyth eventually returned with news that the operation had appeared to go well but I was not out of danger. I was to be transferred to ICU but before being moved, David was invited to see me.

He recalled that it was like walking into a war zone. Blood was all over the floor. I was lying on the table, covered by a sheet, blissfully unaware; with eyes that were still taped shut and a ventilator quietly breathing for me; David kissed my forehead.

When he was ready to leave, he was quietly led away to a spare hospital room to sleep.

When they finished I felt numb. I couldn't even attempt to comprehend what they had gone through. As David said, I had been blissfully unaware; and no matter how hard I tried, I just couldn't accept it had all happened.

Both looked exhausted and I was happy for David to go home to get some sleep. I also knew that deep down a part of him needed to escape from the hospital surroundings, and from what I had just heard, I could understand why (even today he cannot bare hospitals).

As I prepared to settle down for the night, a nurse entered to administer what was to become, a daily injection of a blood-thinning drug to prevent clotting, along with two paracetamol tablets to control my temperature. I knew that my stats would continue to be taken every hour and wondered if I would actually manage to sleep, but surprisingly I was able to drift in and out between checks, and even slept through some!

55

5

Sunday 7th October

I woke around 5am and by 6, the ward was beginning to come alive outside my room. I could hear the tea trolley approaching and soon a chirpy lady appeared at the door offering me a cuppa.

Various nurses popped in and out, what for, I cannot remember, but it's certainly true that when you're in hospital, they like to start the day early!

Believe it or not I was bored. I missed David and although there was a window on my left, all I could see was the sky. On my bedside cabinet to my right was my mobile phone. David had brought it in for me to ring him at any time; so that's precisely what I did, except it was so early I gave him a fright as he thought it was the hospital with some more bad news. We talked briefly but I soon hung up as he was still in bed, trying to get some rest.

As I sit here thinking back, the one common factor that seems to stick in my mind is how quickly time seemed to pass when I was in my room. You would think it would drag by as I had no TV, books, magazines etc, but every half hour or so, staff would pop in and out; and in what seemed like a very short while, David arrived. He had with him the Sunday papers and I was grateful not only to see him, but to have something to do.

He also had with him my little blue overnight bag, only it wasn't quite as full as I remembered.

This was yet another moment in time when I came to realise how hard my being in hospital was for David as he had had to trawl through the contents, removing all items relating to and packed specifically for baby.

*

When I had first arrived onto "Delyth" the day before, a menu card had been given to us. It was for me to choose what breakfast, lunch and dinner I wanted out of the few choices listed. As I did not have much of an appetite, David would help me make my selections; and over the course of the week, it soon became apparent that apart from breakfast (of which I had the same every day), I did not find hospital food very appetising - not because of the quality, which on the whole was very good; I just wasn't hungry.

Breakfast arrived; Rice Crispies and a small tub of orange juice. Little did I know that I was about to embark on a new fetish as the refreshing taste of the juice awoke my taste buds and by the time I finished I was craving more. It soon became apparent that water alone would not satisfy my thirst; thankfully the trolley lady was sympathetic to my plight and would often drop by with unwanted tubs that I horded. I felt like a squirrel ferreting away his stash of acorns!

By mid morning my temperature had spiked, but it was felt that this was due to the fact that my milk had come, which of course was only natural as I had had a baby, regardless of the outcome.

However it was a sensation I did not take too kindly to as not only did I feel hot, but my boobs were solid and very uncomfortable. It was discussed if I should be prescribed a drug to dry the milk up, but in the end it was agreed that as I would not be breastfeeding, my body would resolve the issue on its own. For now, cold flannels were put on my chest and a fan brought in to cool me down.

Again I have to stress how marvellous all the staff were. Such care was taken when having to wash me and change my bed. Numerous cups of tea were offered to David – nothing was too much trouble. They sensed too how anxious I was about my recovery and therefore would assure me that everything was ok each time they came to check my stats.

David and I whiled away the hours reading the Sunday papers – not really talking except to read to each other details of an article that we found interesting.

It's funny looking back as apart from the various drains and drips I was attached to (oh and the fact that I was laid up in a hospital bed!); it seemed like any other Sunday.

In the afternoon my family visited; as did Mike and Wendy, Mark and Camilla (having driven from their home just outside London). Poor Camilla, she had bought me a huge bouquet of flowers, but that was before I had announced I didn't want any flowers (God knows why!) so she left it at home; trouble was she had learnt that my brother had bought me some (he never listens to me); and as she didn't want to arrive empty handed she had called into a local garage. I don't think the few stems she managed to acquire, quite stood up to the fine selection now residing on her dining room table!

I think it's fair to say they too were a little shocked when they first saw me (as all my visitors were) - heavy bruising was developing up the inside of my lower arms, which was a direct result of the battering my veins had taken when trying to get "lines" into me in theatre. But I was still smiling and seeing everyone lifted my spirits even more.

The hospital were very kind in that normal visiting hours were not being applied so people could come and go pretty much as they pleased, as long as the visits were kept short; but at times I would find it all too much and lapse off into a sleep, regardless of who was there.

With so many for company, David had taken the opportunity to grab some fresh air and on his return he had presents for me - a personal CD player, a flask of hot tomato soup (my favourite), but best of all, a new portable TV with built in video.

As you can imagine having my own TV was fantastic for all the obvious reasons; but for David it meant more than that as it gave him piece of mind. It was important to know that when he was not there, television, films and music would help distract me from my thoughts; he was worried that I would be left lying in bed with nothing but the memories of the previous day's events to keep me company.

I guess you've noticed that I still have not made mention of Joseph and to be truthful any thought of him had not entered my head, apart from when I had first awoken in ICU.

That sounds very harsh doesn't it; and now as I look back it leaves me feeling ashamed as a mother.

However I was not out of the woods yet; my health had become the hospitals number one priority, and whilst I was still attached to oxygen masks, drips and drains, I could not focus on anything else.

Every time something was unplugged or un-hooked I felt as though I was winning. When the monitoring of my stats moved from every half hour to every hour; I could relax a little.

I had a husband who was living a nightmare. Whilst I knew minute to minute what was happening, he was at home wondering if the phone was about to ring. David was my priority and I had made a conscious decision very early on that this was not going to destroy our marriage. I had to be strong and was intent on being so.

6

Monday 8th October

At around 9:30 David arrived but before coming to see me, the midwife on duty, Wendy, wanted to talk to him.

As soon as he entered my room he said that it had been suggested we should have Joseph brought to us. I just nodded and agreed; it was as simple as that.

It was my first realisation that he was here, in the same hospital – we had had a baby; and for the first time since arriving over four days ago, we were about to meet him. I rang mum and delayed them coming to see me. I didn't explain why.

For a while neither David nor I spoke. He sat beside me holding my hand, I lay in bed; both straining our ears for the sound of the midwife's footsteps that would signal his approach.

The door opened; it was the tea trolley. We politely declined then David popped out to ask if we could remain undisturbed. A note was put on the door.

Time passed. I don't know how long, it felt like forever. Then the door opened once more, and slowly a small, woven Moses basket started to come into view. My lungs seemed to stop working, David immediately stood up and we both began to cry. Blinking back the tears, smiling, we looked upon our son.

He was perfect. Not small, 8lb 6ozs. He was beautifully wrapped in a blanket, with a small knitted hat. All we could see was his face. David gently stroked his cheek and kissed him.

I felt for his foot through the blanket and peeked under the hat in wonder at his tiny ears. David had gently warned me that he was cold; as I didn't want this to be my lasting memory of him I didn't touch him directly; I never got to feel how soft his skin was.

Wendy (the midwife) asked if I wanted to hold him, but I said no - he looked peaceful and cosy; I actually thought that I didn't want to wake him.

That one single moment in time, became the biggest regret of my life that has broken my heart over and over again. I never held my child. I didn't feel his weight in my arms. I didn't hold him close to me.

For this reason alone I cannot bring myself to hold a baby; I don't think I ever will for fear of the floodgates opening and years of sadness and emptiness pouring out. I have become an expert in controlling my emotions concerning Joseph; using every means possible, from laughter to rejection. I can become very matter of fact about the whole experience to the point that people think I can't be that upset over it.

But there are moments, sometimes many lumped together, when I escape to a quiet corner of the house in the middle of the night and cry until I am drained of every ounce of energy and breath. Until my chest hurts and my throat is raw...

Wendy went to excuse herself from the room but we insisted she stay. We wanted to share the joy and pride we felt in our son with her, even though Joseph had died, we felt the same exhilaration as any other parent.

I don't know how long we had him with us before he left; and once he was gone we never saw him again. Nor did anyone else. Our role as parents, although now limited, did not stop us from wanting to protect him; to the extent that we decided he would not be seen by any member of our family. Eventually we gave each Grandparent a photograph.

We also reversed our decision to have an autopsy. When we had first been approached following our arrival at hospital, it seemed the logical thing to do as we were determined to try again, and needed to know if there was some inherent problem. Now though, it seemed pointless. I couldn't have more babies, and the one we did have was not about to be subjected to the knife.

We don't regret having done so; and although without one, the hospital could not be certain of the cause of death, we both knew that no-one had been to blame. For some reason, that as yet had not become apparent, our son had died. We knew we had to accept that or become bitter and twisted.

*

I had barely had time to take in seeing Joseph, before I became the main focus again as Wendy soon returned to remove the blood drain that protruded from my abdomen. She warned me that the procedure was a little uncomfortable, so suggested I top up on morphine using my PCA button. She also brought with her some gas & air for me to breathe.

Although a quick procedure that involves pulling out the small tube connecting the drain to the site of the operation, she was certainly right about it being uncomfortable.

In fact the word "little" was an understatement. It wasn't painful, not that I can remember, it just left me feeling sick. The best I can describe is when you drive over a hump back bridge, and as you descend the other side, your stomach seems to lurch and drop.

It was like that only a hundred times worse; at one stage I wondered if my remaining organs were going to pass through the tiny incision, attached to the end of the tube. But as quickly as it had begun, it was over and the drain was out. I was also taken off the oxygen; although I did miss the bubbles that had soothed me to sleep over the past few nights.

So it was that my mind had switched from the most important moment in my life, back to the sterile environment of the hospital, in the blink of an eye.

*

It was now the afternoon and my parents had arrived. I shared with them that we had seen Joseph, Mum had guessed that was the reason for postponing their earlier visit; and we also explained our decision about not wanting anyone to see him. They understood. I've never asked them how they felt about it; discussing Joseph with them is something that does not some easy.

Whilst they were there, I was visited by Dr Andrew Bagwell. I was so glad to see him as his voice had kept me alive when being rushed into theatre. I had asked if he would visit as I wanted to thank him.

He was glad to see that I had greatly improved since the last time he had been with me. Mum, as mums do, asked a question that I had not even considered, "Had her heart stopped?" The answer was no; although it had been a battle to stop my organs from shutting down.

Through listening to him, it became apparent to them how close they had come to losing their daughter. Up until now we had not discussed with my parents the details of the operation in full. My Dad sat very quietly as my Mum hugged and kissed Andrew (honestly, your parents never stop embarrassing you!)

My parents visit was short lived; for them it was comfort enough to just pop in every day to say hello, and check everything was ok.

When left alone, David and I settled down to watch a video, amongst the films that had been brought in was "Monty Python's: The Life of Brian".

I remember drifting in and out of sleep to the sound of John Cleese as a Roman soldier, chastising Brian for his use of Latin verbs.

The film has since become a memory trigger; although I still watch it now and again, I don't enjoy it as much.

*

Deb's stopped by. It was her birthday. I felt awful that we hadn't got her a card. Naturally she wasn't upset. She stayed for a while and chatted about the gardening she had been doing. When I started to drift off again she took this as her cue to leave.

I received five more visitors that evening: Linda from work, who had brought with her a lovely card that everyone had signed. Maria, a close friend, she brought white freesia's. With her was Rod, one of Dave's oldest friends (he worked for Maria's husband, Simon).

Later Sarah, my close friend (she eventually went on to marry Rod and have baby Oliver!) and finally Heather, who I had gone to college with.

The hospital staff were not happy. They called David out and told him that I was becoming too exhausted.

When Heather left they checked my stats. My temperature was right up. A doctor was called to ensure that everything was ok. After a tense few minutes, we were assured that it was, but I was to curb my visitations.

I had been officially told off.

7

Tuesday 9th October

Today it was suggested that my drips be temporarily disconnected and I take a shower. Not only to feel fresh, but to get me out of bed as I had literally been on my back for over 5 days.

My room was only across the corridor from the bathroom so I assumed that the short walk would not prove too difficult.

Wrong!

It took two nurses, one either side, just to get me there. David's job was to support me from behind as well as carry my catheter (nice!). I swear my legs had turned to jelly. I couldn't stand unaided, and when I did walk, it was more of a shuffle. By the time I got there, I felt exhausted and was grateful to sit down in the shower chair.

Now as I have said before, you lose all sense of modesty in hospital and I was quite happy having a nurse on hand in case of trouble. She helped me with my gorgeous hospital gown (very flattering!) and passed me my shower gel and shampoo. (I had packed a bottle of coconut shower gel in my bag - the smell became instantly lodged in my memory to such an extent that I had to ask my mum to stop using a similar product when they stayed over once, even though it was years later).

The feel of the warm water washing away any remaining traces of blood from my hair and body was amazing. I had never before appreciated just how uplifting a shower could be and by the end

I felt ten times better in myself. To add to my exhilaration I was allowed to wear my own nightgown. Once my hair was combed I was shuffled back to my room.

On the approach to my bed I noticed for the first time that there was a mirror on my bedside cabinet. I asked if I could look into it, I needed see myself, I think to confirm that it was in fact me that was living this surreal existence.

My breath caught in my chest as I stared at a face that although looked familiar, could not possibly be mine - it was swollen and badly bruised... could that be me? Where my CVC line entered my neck was a mass of deep purple bruising mixed with bloodshot skin, which stretched up and over the side of my jaw.

My eyes looked sunken. The only thing that I recognised was my hair, short, dark, with a slight wave. What must I have looked like when I had emerged from theatre?

But I did not have time to dwell on my looks as I was in for a treat – a wheelchair had been brought in so that David could take me for a spin; with my catheter hidden under a blanket, we started with a push down the mile long 1st floor corridor and back again.

But wait, it gets better; as the hospital is over 100 years old, we stopped to admire the Victorian craftsmanship of the original sash windows and many other, fascinating, architectural delights... umm, very stimulating - by the end of the tour I was hungry for more(?!)

Feeling reckless we made a break for freedom courtesy of a lift to the ground floor where we soon located an exit door to the outside world. David was feeling a little too playful and decided to run down the exit ramp, which was not a good move as my blanket caught in the wheels and I jolted to a halt. My heart stopped as I wondered if I was about to be catapulted out of my chair - I laughed nervously, then told him off.

The sky was blue and although it was early October, the air was warm. To feel the light breeze on my face was wonderful as was the smell of fresh air. We didn't stay too long outside and soon returned back.

Simon, Maria's husband was coming to see me, but first my catheter was to be removed. The procedure took only a few moments and it felt good to get back another part of my body. At least that's what I thought.

Just before Simon was due to arrive, I was advised to try and have a wee, just to make sure everything was working ok. Why shouldn't it be? I wondered. After all I was toilet trained (and had been for some years now). Plus with the amount of fluid I had been passing, I knew that my kidneys were working.

David helped me out of bed but as I stood up gravity took over and I basically peed on the floor! I knew I was doing it but I couldn't stop. I was mortified. The nurses came to help and assured me that having had a catheter for so long, I would have to work on my muscles to gain control.

But it had only been a few days! How could I lose thirty years of experience in just a few days? And more importantly how long was it going to take?

I changed my nightdress and slippers and climbed back into bed feeling quite upset. How was I to get to a toilet in time if every time I stood up... Niagara Falls?

The nurses soon answered that question when they returned with a commode chair. For the first time since my admission, I felt embarrassment.

But the reality was I needed it so I quickly learned to live with it and for the remainder of my stay, I had my own "en suite" toilet close to hand.

At least it proved useful for additional visitors as I had had only one visitors chair in my room up until then!

8

Wednesday 10th October

Mum and Dad had decided to travel back to London. I was doing well so they were happy to return home for a short while.

Before they came to say their goodbyes, I had shuffled off for a shower; and instead of settling back into bed on my return I elected to sit in my visitor chair. I wanted to greet them with a positive image; and it pleased them immensely to see me "up and about".

My brother and Trish also returned home. In a way I was glad that my family were regaining some form of normality, but it also made me feel a little sad as it was becoming apparent how far removed from a normal life David and I were.

Once they had gone, I prepared myself for the removal of half of my stitches - now that was one weird experience! When Helen (midwife) came in to perform the procedure, I was surprised to learn that staples had in fact been used to close the incision, and that she would be using a form of staple extractor to remove them!

As I lay on my bed, I was aware of a mild sensation below, but I can confirm it was not in the least bit painful. When she finished she helped me sit up; only thing was I didn't want to - what if my tummy popped open? I felt very vulnerable.

Trying not to laugh, Helen explained that the staples she had left were more than enough to stop that from happening and besides, there was a whole raft of internal stitches in place that were doing a sterling job of keeping my insides from falling out.

Now you may snigger, but worse was to follow, much to my embarrassment. When Mr Roberts paid me one of his regular visits, I had asked him what exactly, had been removed.

He explained that although my uterus was gone, my ovaries remained, and as such I would continue to experience all the sensations of a monthly cycle, except without the stomach cramps or blood loss.

"But what would happen to the eggs that would continue to be released?", he advised they would travel along my fallopian tubes, where they would hit a dead end and be absorbed by my body (after all, they too were just another form of body cell). This I understood; but what was holding everything in place? He looked a little confused - so I explained myself.

You see, when studying biology and the female reproductive organs in school, I had, on numerous occasions, drawn a diagram of a uterus with a fallopian tube sticking out at right angles from either side (ending in a couple of ovaries); and to complete the picture, a vagina – but here's where the problem lay; as students, we were never shown what these organs were attached too!

If my uterus had been removed (which according to my diagrams was central to the whole process) what was stopping my fallopian tubes (complete with ovaries) from floating about in the void that now existed? (I told you I was about to seriously embarrass myself!) The answer was simple; my tubes were safely attached to other areas within my body. (Needless to say, I have kept my obvious lack of biological knowledge quiet....at least until now!)

*

It was time for another outing, only this time we were to explore the ground floor where we came across a café.

As I was starting to get my appetite back and David fancied a cup of tea, we stopped by, which proved a challenge as the layout did not really take into account people in wheelchairs. Don't get me wrong, it was fully equipped with low counters etc, it's just that there were some very nice ornamental plants and screens placed in such a way that they restricted David's ability to manoeuvre my wheelchair.

But we got there in the end and found an empty table tucked away in the corner.

As we sat I watched people come and go (I'm a great people watcher) and smiled as some, like me, were in their night clothes.

Then a pregnant woman came in. She was quite far gone and as she stood in line holding her purse I could feel a kind a panic begin to rise. She was the first expectant mother I had come across since my arrival almost a week before. Suddenly I had to go.

Trying not to sound how I felt I asked David to wheel me out, but I guess I did a poor job of hiding it as he immediately jumped up and began to navigate his way.

We must have looked like a comedy act as David turned my chair this way and that, trying to avoid crashing into the plants, and instead almost taking one of the ornamental screens with us!

*

I pass the same café every time I attend hospital for a blood test as the haematology department is a little further along, and every time I find myself glancing in – like a moth to the flame I can't ever pass by without doing so.

Vividly I can see us making a bolt for it like some bizarre "out of body" experience, even after all these years - yet another memory I can't erase.

9

Thursday 11th October

It was exactly one week to the day when I had first arrived at hospital to have our baby but I didn't feel any different to the day before, or the day before that.

In fact the only concern I had was for an area of my neck that still felt numb; just under my chin and slightly to the left. A doctor was called to investigate and I was told it was due to my central line having "scratched" a nerve, that would eventually heal in time (it never did and I now find that spot strangely comforting to touch when I'm deep in thought.)

David and I watched TV, but as late evening approached I began to feel quite emotional and for the first time since waking in ICU, I began to grieve over the loss of our son. I guess it was because I could associate time being equal to exactly one week before; for David it was too hard to bare and he felt compelled to leave.

*

Now you may want to criticise him for doing so, but before you do consider this. All throughout the week, whilst I had been safely tucked up in hospital surrounded by a team providing me with 24 hour support; David had been making all the necessary arrangements for our son's funeral.

Unbeknownst to me, he had already attended the offices of the local registry office to record Joseph's death – a very surreal experience for what was, until 7 days before, an excited and expectant father.

Every night he would call into friends on his way home, desperate to delay the inevitable; to return to a house that was empty of life.

When you add this to the trauma of my time in theatre and ICU, I think he can be forgiven for buckling under the strain. But he did not leave me alone; before he left he asked that a midwife sit with me. I lay in bed, staring out the window and began to cry with guilt; I had allowed our child to die.

Thurs 11/10/01: Caroline tearful tonight. Relaying events of one week ago. Wanting to talk about everything.

The midwife on duty sat with me whilst I cried. She was very supportive and would not leave my side until I had exhausted myself enough that I slept.

*

It is important that you realise just how lucky we were to have such amazing individuals sharing this experience with us. The staff that looked after me were exemplary in every way. If it had not been for their honest approach to the situation I would not have recovered as quickly, mentally, as I did physically.

To have people around you, trained professionals, who were not afraid to show emotion, meant the world to us. We felt as though we were constantly surrounded by friends.

When Wendy shared our time spent with Joseph, David hugged her in comfort as she too was crying.

A nurse, who had been in theatre with me, rang in as soon as she had awoken from her shift that night; asking for news of my condition - it just never occurred to me that hospital staff would ever take their work home with them. I had always assumed that the only way to cope with the daily stresses of hospital life was to block it out; but how wrong I was. Especially as the same nurse approached me when I was finally discharged, to say goodbye and wish me luck.

And it didn't stop there. Months later I was told how a hospital staff member had driven to our local Tesco store to buy a baby grow to dress Joseph in, the night he was born.

You see David and I had not thought to bring anything with us when we had first arrived at the hospital except for my nightdress & slippers; and as I was in theatre, and David somewhat preoccupied; they had taken it upon themselves to ensure that our baby was cared for. Apparently they couldn't bear the thought of him being dressed in any of the second hand clothes normally kept as back up by the maternity ward.

Every time I look at Joseph's photograph, taken just after he was born, I think of them, even though I do not know their name.

10

Friday 12th October

0945: Caroline appears brighter this morning, up and about. Celebrating her birthday today. Felt that everything re-lived yesterday, very tearful yesterday. Wound mainly comfortable, remaining clips to be removed. Observations stable. Husband David present.

As I turned 32 I found myself in the one place I had wanted to avoid on my birthday - fate has a funny way of messing with your plans.

I was feeling positive again, and keen to open the post that David had brought with him. Amidst the birthday cards was one sympathy card. David was mortified. He had been so careful in trying to differentiate the two, but it was ok, I told him.

There were presents too; I can't remember exactly, but my brother's certainly stuck in my head; a large bottle of Harvey's Bristol Cream – my favourite Christmas drink!

Chocolates were in abundance, which I opened straight away and shared with all the medical staff who came in (I had many visitors that day!)

Outside the sky was blue and the sun warm. After I had showered, David took me for my customary "once around the block". We sat together outside the main entrance of the hospital and chatted, me in my chair, David on a wooden bench beside me.

With the sun warming my face, I began to talk about wanting to go home; but David had already observed the tell tale signs that I was more like my old self when he had caught me pottering about my room that morning, rearranging the photo's he had brought from home; as well as the vases of flowers on my bedside cabinet.

Apparently, "rearranging" is a habit I have that I'm not always aware of; so we posed the question of my discharge to the midwife on duty when we returned to my room – she promised she would find out if a date had been set.

Today would also see the return of Helen to remove my remaining staples, drip and central line. Neither caused me any discomfort and David was relieved to see the last of the needles removed.

He hadn't quite got over the midweek crisis of having to re-locate my drip when the vein in my right arm gave up; even though the doctor on call tried flushing it through.

The problem was that many of my veins were too "weak" to take a drip, but eventually one was found in my left arm. It took a couple of goes to position the needle and I assured David that it didn't hurt; it just looked worse.

Helen raised the subject of a post mortem with us. According to my medical notes, we had given our verbal consent, but it was also noted that we had not in fact signed the appropriate forms. She wanted to know if our feelings had changed. They had.

Joseph was our son and although he had died, we were fiercely protective of him.

As my chances of having more children were non-existent, there seemed little point in trying to establish why he had died. We knew we would not find any comfort in knowing. We had to simply accept it had happened; nothing we could say or do was going to change events past.

*

For me having to think about the reason why awoke deep rooted beliefs I did not know existed.

I'm Catholic, and until that point in time, I firmly believed that as a non-practicing Catholic, my exposure to the whole foundation of Catholicism had not impacted heavily on me.

Yes I believe in God and yes I married in a church, but those were all "run of the mill" events born out of being raised a Catholic. As an adult I chose not to attend church as I believed (and still do) that you can talk to God from where ever you are. He does not need a building to hear you.

When Joseph died I did not cast aside my religion as you would expect, but instead embraced it and drew strength from it.

Even now I still hold true to my belief that there was a purpose to Joseph's death and trust God to know what He is doing with that great plan of His (although I do struggle at times).

The only question I have is why if He was short of an Angel, did He have to take ours?

I was asked by Helen if we had considered having children by other means; already the idea of adopting had flickered through my mind (although I had not shared this with David).

Surrogacy I knew immediately was out of the question; even though between the two of us, we had all the ingredients (we were just short of an oven); but there was no way I was going to watch another woman "grow" my child. If I could not carry, I certainly didn't want anyone else to.

*

You could argue that it was too soon to have someone ask us this, but it made us start thinking about looking to the future and rebuild our hope of becoming a family.

11

Going home

The weekend was uneventful as by now I required minimum attention. Everything had been removed and the medical team were happy to allow my own internal repair system to take over.

By Sunday I was stir crazy. If consent was not given to allow me home, I would have tried to escape. Thankfully, however, plans for operation "knotted bed sheet" did not come to fruition as I was told I would be discharged first thing Monday morning.

David was ecstatic and left early on the Sunday evening to prepare a bag for me (and I suspect have a bit of a tidy up!); as he left, I noted it was the first time I had seen him with a spring in his step.

When he returned on Monday he was super early and itching to get going. I on the other hand wanted to say my goodbyes to everyone, which irritated David somewhat as I had so many to thank. Don't get me wrong, he wasn't being rude; he just wanted to leave hospital, never to return.

To dress in my own clothes felt quite weird and at the time I believed myself to have lost weight and look quite slim (I blame the drugs!) But later when I referred back to a photograph my parents took of me shortly after leaving hospital, the reality was I looked quite bloated.

Whilst saying my goodbyes, David had taken the opportunity to load up the car with all my belongings. When the time came to leave, all I had left to carry was my little blue hospital bag.

Hand-in-hand we left. I was still unsteady on my feet and therefore a slow waddle was all I could manage as we walked out through the same entrance we had arrived at 11 days prior – memories that seemed a lifetime ago from where we were now.

Due to the nature of my wound, I had to place a pillow on my abdomen to protect it from the seatbelt.

As David drove out of the grounds we travelled in silence. Our home was only few minutes by car and as we approached I became overwhelmed with emotion.

This was not the return from hospital I had envisaged. I should have been sat in the back whilst our baby resided in his car seat in the front.

Where were the helium balloons daubed with messages of congratulations?

Before we reached our road, I broke down and cried.

One day at a time

It's difficult to diarise events that occurred following my discharge. So many separate memories, feelings and emotions overlap each other, and when mixed in with the mundane routines of life, to put them in some form of daily order is impossible; as, opposed to writing about being in hospital, they cannot be taken one day following another.

So I have decided to approach those that remain forever etched in my mind under their own, headings - I guess you'd refer to them as little snippets.

Some are long, some exceptionally short, but each as important as the other as they are the foundation on which our lives are now built, and are the reasons for why we do what we do now and how we approach life.

12

Walking through the door

I felt empty and sad. My mood had completely changed during that short journey from the hospital; as if the cocoon that I had been living in was now gone and I was part of the real world again.

Without the distractions of hospital life I, like David, was forced to face the reality of our situation.

On the kitchen side was a stack of sympathy cards, one of the first things I did was to sit down and read them.

The first card I read was from the Commodore of our local yacht club. It took me back a little as we had not always got along, but none of that mattered anymore and to know that he had thought to send a card filled me with warmth. His was probably one of the most appreciated out of all the cards we received - he died a few years later, but I still think of him.

Everyone was so kind in what they wrote. One couple, whom David had known for years, told us that they too had lost a baby - David was unaware of this. It's funny how something happens and all of a sudden friends say "that happened to me".

I took a deep breath and asked David to help me upstairs to Joseph's room. When I walked in I was struck by how different it looked.

When I had left it was organised and tidy; but now it was crammed full of "stuff" – his pram, car seat (still in its plastic cover), Moses basket; all just dumped like some sort of dusty old bric-a-brac shop – I can still smell the newness of it all.

I sat on the rocking chair and just stared at everything; David was with me but there was an uncomfortable silence. I could sense he felt uneasy being there; as if we were in a room that did not belong to us and we must leave.

I don't recall how long I sat, nor what we did afterwards - in fact, I don't recall much of my first day.

13

Doing what has to be done

It was on Tuesday morning (the day after my return) that a chap from the funeral home called to finalise arrangements. He was very nice and appreciated my condition; so offered to come to the house later that evening.

Whilst in hospital, David had been planning Joseph's funeral with the help of our friend Simon. He has a stonemasons business and had recommended a funeral director based in the neighbouring town. The date was set for the following Monday, 22nd October; but here's the rub, only the Mother of the child can sign the forms to purchase and own the grave – I know in my heart that if David could have shouldered the responsibility he would have done so.

Prompted by his phone call, I began to think about what I wanted to go in the coffin - I knew immediately. Joseph was to be wrapped in a hand crocheted shawl, which had been made and sent by my old next door neighbour in London; and a small blue bunny that I had bought from Mothercare during my last outing to the shops.

I remember trying to decide if I should go with the lemon as we did not know the sex of our baby; but something inside guided me to buy blue – I guess my instincts were right about one thing.

*

I don't remember the name of the funeral director but I do remember that he was even nicer in person than he had been on the phone. He expressed to us his deepest sympathies and his manner was so gentle.

The forms that I had dreaded so much were produced. Staring down at them I could not believe that I was actually about to "purchase" a grave for my child. The turmoil I felt inside was overwhelming and my hand shook as I signed.

As for our choice of coffin, it was assumed that we would want white but I'm afraid I caused him a problem as although he had ordered one, I actually wanted a normal wooden casket - white just seemed so predictable. We were assured that the change would be made.

When the time came for him to leave, I produced a Tesco bag (of all things) that contained the shawl and bunny. We were asked if we wanted to visit Joseph one last time, but we declined. We had said our goodbyes at the hospital.

If you want to know now how I feel about our decision – I would have to refer to it as regret number two.

Also on that Tuesday the vicar who had married us, called by unannounced. When I opened the door and saw him standing there, I burst into tears and hugged him.

Over a cup of tea we discussed the service we wanted. It was to be by the graveside with only ourselves, our parents, brothers (and wives of course) in attendance. We also wanted Richard and Debs to be there as they were to have been Joseph's

Godparents. I asked if Rev. Cox would visit Joseph at the funeral home and bless him, before the coffin was sealed; he was happy to do so.

*

And the remainder of Joseph's processions? It was with a cold heart that David and I simply shoved everything into black plastic bags and put them up in the attic. The cot was dismantled, as was the changing table; and the pram that had been lent to us by my brother, put away until it could be returned.

We couldn't afford to be emotional and in no time at all the nursery that had once held all our hopes and dreams, resembled an empty box room. The very next day David would buy a tin of bland paint to cover the multi coloured walls.

New furniture would fill the void and we would purposely leave the door open at all times; to remind ourselves that the room behind it was just another space in the house.

In time I would sort through everything and neatly lay it out in an old trunk, given to me by my parents.

Every piece of clothing has been kept; every soft toy we bought.

The scribbles I wrote after waking up in hospital are with them, so too is the video footage (on cassette) from the camcorder we bought and the photos from my scans.

I even have a single feeding bottle and the remainder of a roll of wallpaper that was part of nursery's décor.

The car seat, bath etc, I gave away. The cot and changing table we held onto (they were eventually sold).

The Moses basket I still have. It was bought when my brother was born and is made up of a woven wicker basket on a stand (like a cradle) of twisted cane. It had been kept in our old attic back home in London, until the first of my brother's kids had arrived and my mum (who was a tailor by trade) re-lined it. When Nigel and Trish no longer needed it I asked to have it for our baby.

Now it lives in our attic, still with the covers on that mum made afresh for our son.

It's partially wrapped in a black bin liner. I can look at it, but it can hurt; however I can't bear to give it up. It's a family piece.

14

Being the bearer of bad news

We live in a relatively small town and you are always guaranteed to meet someone you know - during one trip to the local supermarket we bumped into a good friend of ours, Jamie Morgans.

Jamie has a daughter who, ironically, had just celebrated her first birthday the day Joseph was born, Oct 4th.

As we approached each other in the aisle David grew tense; he was unsure if Jamie knew anything, but we were greeted with a warm smile and a big hug that spoke volumes.

In a bizarre twist of fate, Jamie had only just come from a meeting at the lifeboat station where he had asked mutual friends of ours if it was time yet to "wet the baby's head", only to be told that things had not exactly gone according to plan.

We said our goodbyes and continued with our shopping. As we perused the isles, one or two pregnant women passed and I could feel my breath catch in my chest. David remained ever close.

After the supermarket, we headed for the high street – I can't remember what David needed to do. At first he insisted that we stick together but I told him to go on ahead and meet me at the bank; as it is a small local branch and I know the counter staff well, I knew as soon as they saw me they would ask about Joseph and I wanted to spare David the pain of having to explain.

As expected, when I walked in the two ladies looked at me and smiled; keeping my voice calm I told them the sad news. As their smiles faded I felt awful.

This was my first experience of having to break our news to someone and I didn't like it. I felt as if I was pulling the rug out from under them. I quickly started to console them with words such as "I'm sorry" and "don't worry, it's ok"... it was like some kind of weird role reversal; with me actually apologising for breaking such news.

David walked in and knew instantly what had happened as he was use to seeing the same expression every time he too had had to tell someone. His look of concern however was directed at me, but I assured him I was ok as we left the bank.

I felt awful; I had just ruined someone's day. But should I feel like this? I guess so.

Worst thing is there's no way to avoid it. Even now when I'm in a situation where by I have to explain a little about what happened; I start to shift uncomfortably in my seat and avoid the eyes of the person I am talking to. It's as if I have some terrible secret.

And what if I'm in the company of a pregnant woman? If it's someone I don't know very well and she's gushing on about the wonders of little kicks and ultrasound (as I did), then I just nod.

If it's someone whom I know but haven't told, that's more difficult.

If I let slip something I remember from my pregnancy quizzical looks are thrown at me - how could I have experience of such things if I can't have children? But that's just it; I did; except how do I explain where Joseph is to a pregnant woman?

And if someone doesn't know and says "do you think you'll have children" and I say I can't, they then feel awful for having asked.

Of course I could just come out with it, very matter of fact; but of course you don't; especially if David is around - he can't bear being reminded.

We just want to be normal and have normal conversations instead of harbouring some deep dark, terrible secret; or at least that how it feels.

15

Joseph's funeral

The time had originally been set for 11:30am but was later altered to 3:30pm. This meant we had most of the day to think about what was to happen; we felt very sad but I was determined not to break down and cry. David and I would be dignified and strong for our boy.

Whilst in the shower the door bell had rung. When I went downstairs David told me that our flowers had arrived; a small display of white roses and two single red rose stems.

But where were they? David had put them straight in the downstairs toilet. He tried to convince me that it was because it was the coldest room; but I knew he just couldn't face them.

Later that morning Mark and Camilla arrived and remained with us until it was time to leave for the cemetery. They were a welcome distraction.

My parents were staying once more at Michael and Wendy's house. Nigel and Trish in a B&B just down the road – no one was to stay at our house and it had been arranged that after the funeral we would all go back to Mike and Wendy's for "tea and sandwiches".

When the time came to leave, I sat in the front whilst David drove; Mark and Camilla followed in their car as they were returning home later that day and would need it with them.

We drove first to Mike and Wendy's as their house was across from the cemetery - every one, except David and I were to walk.

As David drove through the cemetery gates the funeral director was waiting to escort us to the grave. David parked behind him and got out of the car to shake hands.

After a short discussion David began to walk back to the car but as the funeral director prepared to drive ahead for us to follow, he at first moved to retrieve something from the boot of his car. As he opened the hatch back I saw Joseph's coffin.

It was a huge shock and suddenly I could feel my chest tighten and the tears well up – but I wanted to be strong and somehow managed to suppress my grief.

I must have thought that somewhere there was a hearse parked waiting; but as we were to have a graveside ceremony, I can only conclude that a hearse was not necessary.

It was a dreadful moment for me. The last time I had seen my son he had been gently wrapped and placed in a Moses basket, but now here he was just lying in a box in the boot of someone's car. On reflection I feel guilty and ashamed that we had not taken more care over his arrangements and wonder how, as parents, we had let this happen.

The cemetery is not a big place, and Joseph's grave was only a few hundred meters from the main gate, through the arch and just past the old Sunday school building. As we turned the corner Reverend Cox came into view.

We also saw three more men in attendance; two were from the funeral home, the other was the cemetery caretaker.

They kept a respectful distance and smiled sympathetically as we approached. Within moments our families, Richard and Deb's, had joined us.

Reverend Cox handed out a leaflet that outlined the ceremony. He had spent time writing a special service filled with prayers and words of comfort. It was to last about fifteen minutes.

When Joseph's coffin was carried past us to the grave side, Mike seemed to buckle and Mark took his arm. I guess it was a shock to everyone to see such a small casket; but you must also remember that this was the first time family and friends had seen him and been close.

Here was the proof that Joseph Michael Youde existed. He was real. Here was our son whom we cherished and were about to say goodbye to. Three weeks ago I had been at home eagerly awaiting his arrival... so much had gone wrong in such a small space of time.

David and I stood proud as Reverend Cox continued with the service. When it was over, Joseph was slowly lowered into the ground.

We moved forward to throw each of our red roses. Earth was scattered by all those in attendance, including the caretaker.

It was over. As everyone departed, David and I hugged each other. We stood for a short while; and then hand in hand, silently walked away.

The weather was dry. I was still weak hence the need to have the car to drive the short distance back to Mike and Wendy's.

We parked as everyone was arriving. On entering the house we seemed to split into two groups, the girls in the lounge, the boys in the kitchen (I suspect that's where the beer was!)

What we spoke about, I don't know; probably just idle chit-chat.

In the kitchen, David was relaying the events of "that night" (as it is often referred to), to my brother.

Nigel had not heard the full story; I'm not sure if he later regretted asking when the full extent of my illness was known; but I can confirm that when I walked into the kitchen later that afternoon, I was given a huge hug!

16

Return to normality

Once the funeral was over David was feeling as if a weight had been lifted. For him, laying Joseph to rest had been the last hurdle. For everyone else it meant slotting back into their normal routine – but we had to rethink ours.

For so long we had begun to plan how we were to cope with having a baby; who would do this, who would do that... these plans were no more.

David returned to work within a few days of the funeral. He was welcomed back with much support. The day to day problems he so often faced and had to resolve were a perfect distraction.

My wound was healing well and my mobility was improving. Each day I would walk (as I could not drive for six weeks) to the local high street that was about a mile from our house.

Without the car I would enjoy aimlessly ambling from one shop to another; the problem was that the only people that seemed to be home on weekdays were the retired, the pregnant and new mothers. I couldn't get away from them.

Time and time again I would have to stop myself from staring at pregnant bumps and if a newborn came my way I couldn't breathe.

I felt as though I was in a bubble screaming but no one could hear me – the world was going about its business regardless of my pain.

I missed Joseph. It was simple. I asked David if he would drive me to the cemetery within a week of the funeral. He promised to do so on the Friday.

When he got home from work he was very quiet - what was wrong?

Gently he explained that he had visited the grave beforehand - he wanted to check everything was ok and that the grave had been neatly maintained; but what faced him instead was a mound of lumpy wet clay minus the flowers. It all looked so cold and impersonal, as if the earth had just been dumped without any thought.

I couldn't believe it. The caretaker wouldn't have thrown anything away and he surely would have taken more care.

As we made the journey I prepared myself for what I was about to see. Hand in hand we walked through the arch. David was right. The mound was there but no flowers.

But wait, the shrub on the corner was closer to the grave than I had remembered... we were standing in the wrong place and the mound of earth was indeed just that! Joseph was buried approximately six feet away. His grave was neat and tidy and there resting on top were the flowers.

We laughed! Not your belly aching, rolling around on the floor laugh, more of a nervous laugh; but all the same it was a release for both of us. How stupid would we look had we continued to pay homage to a pile of wet clay!

It was a peculiar moment in time that, amongst all the sadness, allows us to reflect with a hint of a smile. To others it may seem strange, but that's the weird thing about loss – we each find comfort in some of the most bizarre memories.

*

And as with any loss there is an element of anger that creeps in.

David came home one evening to me crying. He asked me what was wrong. I told him that I had just heard from friends that one of the couples from our antenatal class had recently delivered a healthy baby boy.

I was crying and angry because why them? Why had their baby lived and ours died?

Of course I didn't want their baby to be dead; I just wanted ours to be alive.

David tried to comfort me and said that it was great news. He said we had to focus on the positive, but for now I was wallowing in self pity and jealousy.

Over time my emotions would change and jealously would give way to sadness. I would cry for our son instead of for myself.

17

Drawing a line under 2001

When in hospital David and I talked about and agreed to take a one week break in West Wales. This we did mid November.

We booked a cottage in a small hamlet just outside St David's. It was what we needed.

Every day we would walk and talk. We'd always enjoyed the Pembrokeshire Coastal Path and with my strength and mobility improving all the time, the fresh air and exercise was a welcome relief.

It was also a time for reflection and we both shared moments where our thoughts were of Joseph. Sometimes we'd each walk ahead of the other, just to be alone for a moment or two.

I remember a particular walk on a secluded beach where David wondered off to some rocks that were being lapped by the sea. He stood there for a while, staring into the distance.

With the sun low in the sky and the dramatic rock formations, it was a perfect setting so I took a photo of him silhouetted against the horizon. It's a picture I'm very proud of and one of David's favourites.

Following our return I had an appointment with Mr Roberts. It was my six week check up, but I had requested that extra time would be allowed to discuss with him questions that had arisen since my discharge.

Walking back into the hospital was a surreal experience for both David and I.

As we drove past the main entrance I was instantly transported back to my birthday and could see David and me sitting in the sunshine.

Because of his office location, we did not have to go anywhere near the maternity unit to see Mr Roberts.

As we waited I could sense David was very uncomfortable so I tried to distract him with idle chit chat until it was our turn.

Mr Roberts welcomed us warmly and explained that I would need an examination to ensure everything had healed; there had been talk of the possibility of an operation to correct any minor inaccuracies as the repair had been somewhat frantic at the time, but I was assured it would be nothing to worry about.

We moved to the adjoining room whilst David waited. The exam took moments and the good news was that I had healed well – when told, David was visibly relieved.

Then Mr Roberts spoke about Joseph. He said that the tests run on his blood and the tissue samples from my placenta, gave no indication as to why he had died; but we were ok with that.

By now, we had reached a state of mind that simply accepted that our son had died and there would be no answers – it was the only way we could ever hope to move on as the alternative was to become bitter and twisted. But he did have an answer for why I was so ill.

It was suspected that the drug given to induce my labour had interacted with my own internal chemical system and in short, I had experienced an allergic reaction thus resulting in my uterus going into overdrive (this would explain why I had dilated so quickly).

It was further explained that my uterus started to tear itself in an effort to speed up delivery, but as Joseph was still in situ, he was acting as a kind of "plug" that stemmed the bleeding. Only when he was delivered could the blood be allowed to flow and I began to haemorrhage.

I was described as "unique". In all of his years of experience, Mr Roberts had not come across a case like mine.

I sat in silence. Typical I thought, as the girl who had always been caught out in school for misbehaving (even if I was with a group of classmates that were doing exactly the same), it had to be me!

We shook hands and left with assurances from Mr Roberts that should I ever need to see him, he would always be there.

Over the past eight years he had remained true to his word, but more of that later.

With our meeting over with, David and I returned to focusing on getting through the first year and with him back at work I too needed a distraction so we got a new kitten!

We already had one cat, Bernard; and as David had agreed without hesitation I soon got to work phoning around local vets until I located a litter that had just been handed in.

I chose a small, grey and white female who was to be named Ronald. I know, I know; but you see Bernard was also a girl and somehow the two names matched.

I had a small, defenceless creature that needed me to care for it – I was happy.

*

Time was moving on and without really noticing Christmas was almost upon us. But what is it about Christmas that people who have lost someone find especially difficult? I guess it's because we all know Christmas is about family and sharing gifts (apart of course from the more important aspect of celebrating Jesus' birthday!)

As a parent it's all about the kids and their excitement knowing Santa is on his way. We both knew how hard this was going to be so decided to have a very "grown up" Christmas.

For the first time ever, neither of us celebrated dinner with our family. Instead we booked into a five star hotel at a ridiculous amount of money for a very adult five course meal.

It was modern, non-traditional and most of all child free. Following this we visited Richard and Deb's and happily munched our way through their sweet tin!

But we hadn't forgotten the most important part of the day – visiting Joseph's grave, which was especially difficult and reduced us both to tears.

*

To share with you if I may a little of my past: My mum's dad died suddenly in 1974, he was 59; my father's parents died the following year, three months apart, of old age and, it is suspected of one, a broken heart.

Growing up we lived with my remaining Gran (mum's mum). It had at first been a temporary arrangement, as my parents were in the process of relocating whilst my mum was carrying me; they had wanted to postpone the stresses of buying a new house until after I was born.

What with my arrival and the loss of my Grandparents, we never moved out!

This meant that we spent every Christmas as a family with my Gran; and it also meant that every Christmas Day morning, from as far back as I can remember, we'd visit the graves of each Grandparent to lay flowers.

When I moved from London, I no longer paid my respects in this way as I was living too far away; it was a ritual that I thought was a part of my past.

Since Joseph's death I find myself again visiting a cemetery on Christmas Day morning; and will continue to do so for as long as I live.

Only once did we postpone our visit until Boxing Day; even now I still haven't forgiven myself as it feels as though I abandoned him.

No child should be left alone on Christmas Day, especially by his parents - it is third biggest regret in my life.

*

For New Year we had been invited to join Mark and Camilla, again in West Wales; they had rented a cottage and it was to be our third time of ringing in the New Year with them.

The four of us had first done so at the turn of the Millennium, which we celebrated in Solva - a beautiful harbour village with a fine selection of pubs! We enjoyed ourselves so much that we returned year after year, and true to form we walked the coast line and climbed the hill at Strumble Head - not bad for someone who only weeks before had been lying in ICU!

But this New Year we had found ourselves rounding off the year as it had begun, as of course October 2001 was to have been the start of a new life and new experiences. It made me question whether the last twelve months had really happened - falling pregnant, the loss of my Grandmother, losing Joseph; when I chose to go to bed before midnight no one battered an eyelid. I wasn't fussed on raising a glass to 2001.

18

Returning to work

On January 7th, 2002, I returned to work - I was looking forward to it as it was another step back to normality and was given the option of starting a little later and leaving a little earlier, at least for the first few weeks so as not to exert myself.

In my mind I saw myself waltzing back in where I had left off and simply slotting back in; however I was instead introduced to the temp who had been employed to cover my position. She was to stay for now in order that we could carry out a proper hand over.

I suppose three months away from the job was a long time? For now I was happy just to be back in a routine I knew so well, but by April she was still there.

I worked in a small office that housed three desks comfortably; but with the continued employment of the now pregnant temp, my manager had (without consultation) rearranged things so that a fourth desk could be brought in. It was placed at right angles to mine (this created an "L" shape).

Day after day I would sit at my desk with the temp in front of me, not facing me though – oh no, my view of her was of her left profile.

I was starting to feel uncomfortable and insecure. Not only had my role not been returned to me, but I was in the presence of a pregnant woman who was steadily getting bigger right before my eyes.

My manager dismissed my concerns and he insisted that it was the only place for her to sit. But why was she still employed? And why were there talks about offering her a permanent contract? I had been back full time since the beginning of February and was trying to move on with my life.

Ok I had a few "wobbly" moments in work whereby I would escape to the toilets to have a cry, but that was to be expected; on the whole I tried hard not to let my personal circumstances affect my job or my colleagues (although I must add they were all hugely supportive when I did wobble).

This was not helping. I felt pressure from all sides. I had to work to help pay the mortgage, but I couldn't take seeing her anymore, so I rang my doctor and had myself signed off for a month.

David was naturally concerned as we were both unsure how this action would affect my future position with the company, especially as they already had someone who could step in. As we didn't want to rock the boat, we did not consult a solicitor – in truth, we didn't know what to do.

But David knew I wasn't someone who would take time off with stress for the simplest of reasons; I was stronger than that (or so I thought), therefore he supported me as it was a clear indication that I had reached breaking point.

However my sudden decision was another test of our relationship as it was a stark reminder of what had happened. We both wanted to move on and this whole situation was taken us backwards.

Over the course of the month I contacted my manager pointing out that this was not constructive to my recovery.

I also spoke with the managing director; I think the biggest shock I received was when it was suggested by him that "moving on" should be considered by me as a possibility because "work held many memories for me".

You can read into this what you may... was I considered by them to be an "inconvenience"? An emotional female with issues? Or was it just a kindly piece of advice with no intent meant; but with my state of mind it only added to my worries.

But positives do come out of negative situations (always the optimist), which I was about to find out.

I had been discussing the problem with our close friend Simon - he knew about employees rights because of his own business.

He advised that the actions taken by my company were tantamount to "constructive dismissal" and if you took into account everything I had been through, they were playing a very dangerous game with regards to an employment tribunal.

But I didn't want to sue anybody, I just wanted an end to the whole situation; so it was suggested that I should meet with my manager to explain again how I felt.

I was to drop into conversation the term "constructive dismissal" without actually accusing them of it and see what transpired.

When the month was up I felt nervous on my drive into work. As soon as he saw me my manager invited me in to his office. Over the course of the next hour and a half he sat and listened to my point of view.

As advised by Simon I hinted, without actually accusing them, that I felt I was being forced to resign. I knew immediately it had been the right approach.

My manager was adamant that they did not see me as an "inconvenience"; he said that he did not think the words expressed by the managing director were meant as an indication that they wanted me to leave – but as words of support.

However he did himself suggest that for my own piece of mind maybe I should consider taking a career break before embarking on a new challenge that wouldn't hold any "ghosts".

With a renewed confidence I said that I was not in a position to take a six month break unless supported financially therefore this was not an option (besides, money wasn't important, I wanted to work as I was proud of what I had achieved).

The meeting on the whole was honest and very open. It was also very amicable. I did not feel any resentment or pressure from my manager and I honestly believe that he did not have the slightest inkling how this whole event had affected me emotionally.

He genuinely took on board my words when I explained that I was not only trying to come to terms with the loss of our son, but also the loss of being able to have any more children - something that did not really hit me until six months after my operation. It was like a second bereavement.

As the meeting drew to a close our discussion turned to the temp. He explained that negotiations were in place for the company to be bought out by a larger organisation. This would mean that my job would probably be split and I would need to share my responsibilities.

Following the changes that may occur, he again turned to the subject of taking a career break. He suggested that I may want to consider a new challenge with a new company, and should I wish to do so, the company would be more than willing to support me with a generous redundancy package.

An offer would be made, following talks with the managing director, and we were to meet later to finalise matters.

It had been an interesting day that had begun with my nervousness at returning to work and the unknown; to walking out with my head held high.

When I discussed the day's events with David he acknowledged that the four figure sum offered was a generous proposal and, taking into account the plans for the company, he agreed that I should take this opportunity to close the door on my current job and start afresh, where no one knew me and I could get back to concentrating on my career.

But he also knew that I was not the type to sit around for six months and was confident that it would not be long before I would secure a new job; he was right, it took me six days.

And so I had a new challenge to focus on. I was to leave a job that I had enjoyed for four years, leaving behind friends that had shown me nothing but love and support.

When I eventually left in the June, I was to enjoy a fabulous send off with everyone joining me at my favourite Italian restaurant, including my manager and the managing director (who, incidentally, picked up the drinks bill!).

It was the right move for all the right reasons. Just before I left it was formally announced that the company take over had finally taken place. The original site was soon closed and everyone moved to a bigger location, further away.

My manager would eventually be made redundant; and in time the company would be closed down.

For me I'm just glad that I left on a positive.

19

Family plans

Whilst the struggle with my job threatened to drag us backwards, David and I were taking steps to move forward.

By late January 2002 we had begun to discuss the option of adoption. It was a subject that I spoke tentatively about at first as I knew David was taking a little longer than I to accept the idea, but by early February we had arranged to meet with a family who had adopted two boys.

We knew the husband well and so it was easy for us all to talk openly. It was also a huge step forward as we could again see our vision of being a family becoming a reality and by the end of the evening David and I both agreed that I was to contact our local council for guidance and advice.

Now as anyone who knows me will testify, once I'm onto something I do not drag my heels. The very next day I spoke to the adoption team and a social worker was assigned to us. Within a matter of days we had our first meeting.

She listened to our "story so far". We expressed our concern that we would be seen to be a couple on the rebound, desperate to replace the son we had lost. But nothing could replace Joseph; we simply wanted to be a family.

Sitting back to ponder what we had told her, a moment or two passed before she spoke.

Her initial reaction was that we had just experienced a very traumatic event and she questioned whether we were emotionally ready; but having listened to how we spoke about it (calmly and honestly), rather than focus on the event itself, she was convinced we were coming at this with level heads.

However, it would not be as simple as that; before we could begin the adoption process, she would need to take our case to "panel", (a group of people consisting of social workers, psychologists and adoptive parents, who meet to discuss and grant couples the right to become an "approved adopter") to seek approval to begin working with us.

We understood why this was to be the case and as she left we shook hands in the hope that we would soon begin a new journey.

The news we had hoped for came in a phone call a week later; the panel were happy for us to proceed. So it was that in early February 2002 the process began and if everything went to plan then we should have full approval by early October – how bizarre; exactly one year to the month.

*

I won't bore you with the full details of what was involved with regards to the adoption process, plus I do not want to run the risk of turning anybody off the idea, but I can tell you that if ALL future parents had to undergo the probing questionnaires and background checks we endured, there would be allot less children in the world.

Don't get me wrong, the end result is worth it, but you have to have a lot of patience and learn how to detach yourself emotionally, otherwise you'd give up.

It certainly makes you think about the whole "parent" thing and whether you really want it.

We did and so we persevered and at the end were officially granted the title, "approved adopters". (However there were side affects - as each week got tougher and tougher, David and I both returned to smoking having stopped some years before. After each visit we could be seen disappearing off to the garage for a cigarette. We felt like naughty school children).

But what now?

During the nine month process David and I decided that we wanted a twelve month break before we would consider taking on a child.

We felt we had earned the rest as we had never really stopped to take stock of past events. The adoption process had certainly helped us get through the first year, but it was time to stop now and focus on us.

My initial thought was how we would inform the agency that this was what we wanted to do. I didn't want them to think that after all our/their efforts to gain approval we were throwing it all back in their face SHOULD a child come into the picture.

Besides, we had been told on numerous occasions that the opportunity of being considered for a baby less than one year old (we had been very exact in this) would be few and far between and could take a minimum twelve months – so all in all, everything seemed to be going to plan (at least that's what we thought!)

Regardless of whether children exist in your life naturally or by adoption, they rarely stick to any form of a plan.

Having got through Christmas and New Year, we entered 2003 with no fixed agenda other than to enjoy life.

However in January we received a call – two brothers aged two and nine months, had been taken into care and our file had been put forward as potential parents.

We were pretty shocked as we had not anticipated being contacted so soon regarding one child, let alone two. In fact we didn't know how to respond and so asked instead for a meeting with our social worker. She was pretty surprised by this request and agreed to call by that evening.

We were very honest with her when we expressed our hesitation at taking on two children. Although our original plan had been to have more than one child, two at the same time was more than we had envisaged.

Also, what about this "minimum twelve months" that had been spoken about? Was this to be our one and only shot at parentage and were we about to blow it?

The answer was no. She admired our cautious approach and felt rest assured that we would not jump at the first opportunity without consideration as to whether it was right for us or the children involved.

But all the same it was a hard decision to make when we rejected the proposal – somewhere; two little boys were waiting patiently for a new Mum and Dad. It broke my heart; it still does.

But I couldn't help but worry that we had had "our card marked" and our file would now find its way to the bottom of the pile. It was only natural to think that, however, as we soon learned, that had certainly not been the case.

In the February, having just returned from (another) mid week break in West Wales, an answer phone message from the agency was waiting for us. We were to call them back first thing.

David didn't want to give any thought as to what they had to say; "let's not speculate" were his words. I, on the other hand, had a gut feeling it was involving another child.

I was right. A baby boy was to be placed for adoption. Again our file had been put forward.

That evening I prepared to break the news to David. I knew he wanted to wait a year, but what if this was to be our opportunity; and we missed it?

Expectedly, he did not react with joyous enthusiasm, nor did he rule out the possibility. True to form, he went quiet on me. I knew this to mean that he wanted to be left alone to think about it.

David always takes time to mull over important issues, he's a thinker and you cannot rush him, (in fact he balances me out perfectly as I'm the complete opposite.) All I could do was potter around the house and leave him to his thoughts.

When he did express his views they were
not what I was expecting – he wanted to wait. His
instincts were telling him to take a year off... get
our lives back on track before we launched into
another, emotionally charged situation.

I was upset. My fear was that this was our
chance to be a family, however I knew that I could
not change his mind; at least not tonight.

The next day (Saturday) I went to see
Richard and Debs to share with them the news and
see what they had to say. Naturally they were
pleased and told me we should go for it. But they
knew David too well; if he was not in agreement
then I had much persuading to do.

When I returned home we sat down and each
voiced our feelings about the pros and cons of
taking on this child; I wanted to say yes. My desire
for a child has not waned since losing Joseph and I
couldn't fall pregnant so this was it in my book.

Again David raised the issue of waiting a
year and reminded me that we had both agreed to
this, which was of course true; so was I being
unfair to now pressure him into changing his mind?

He (we) had both been through so much. I
had to concede that it was not unreasonable of him
to want to take time out.

But a glimmer of hope was had when he
later said that we should call our social worker and
again ask her to come over.

She arrived Tuesday evening. I sat quietly
and let David lead. He knew that I was all for it;
and I knew that there was no changing his mind if
he wasn't ready.

He was to make all the decisions tonight and whatever they were I would support him.

Some background on the child was given and again she assured us that our file would not go to the bottom should we decide no.

But David was swaying towards saying yes. I could tell from his tone and the questions he was asking that he was still thinking about it.

Finally, whilst looking at me, he said that a meeting between us and the child's social worker should be arranged. I was ecstatic inside.

But David was still cautious. He was happy to take the next step but he couldn't promise anything. If, after the next meeting, he was not comfortable with the idea, then I was to be prepared for that; but deep down I knew it would all be ok.

David was still reeling from disappointment and didn't want to get his hopes up. Like anyone who has had their heart ripped out, he was protecting himself.

*

When the day finally arrived that we were to meet the child's social worker, I felt sick with nerves, and as someone who has a fear of flying, I can only liken the sensation to one of waiting to board a plane. The hours dragged as I waited to finish work and return home.

After a series of questions and a tour of our house, photos of the child were presented to us (it was love at first sight); we both felt everything had gone well, however we were advised that it would be another week before there would be any news (when she eventually left, we both escaped to the garage for yet another cigarette!)

Now according to procedures, there would be a meeting of Manager's, where it would be recommended that David and I be presented to the courts as potential legal guardians; but the very next evening we received a phone call at around 6pm.

David came into the lounge saying that the social worker we had met was on her way over! We didn't understand it, had we been rejected?

As soon as we opened the door she announced it was good news. She knew what we were thinking and wanted to allay our fears straight away. Apparently a cancellation in someone's diary at work had resulted in all relevant personnel being available to meet and discuss our case. The agency wanted us to know as soon as possible.

We couldn't believe it, it was official - we were going to be parents... however we still had a long way to go.

*

To conclude briefly on this part of our lives, I can tell you that from the night we received the news to the actual placement of our son, took a little over 4 weeks.

Ordinarily it should take a few months but due to his age and the need to settle him as quickly as possible, we had to move fast.

So at this stage I think it only right to thank a few people:

Vicky (HR Manager) - without your reassurance and understanding the whole idea of the company supporting me in having to take 6 months off at such short notice would have seemed incomprehensible, especially when you bear in mind I had not been in my new job a year! Added to this, is the continued support of the Directors and my work colleagues that, as a full time mum, continues to this day.

And we couldn't have wished for better Foster Parents (who for the purposes of my book, will have to rename anonymous). From the moment we started the bonding process you made it clear that we were "mum & dad". From changing nappies to feeding, you helped us every step of the way.

*

In less than a year the courts awarded David and I full guardianship – we had made it at last; a little over 3 years from when I first fell pregnant; we had a son.

20

A year to the day

First anniversaries are always the hardest as up until that point the person you are grieving for was alive twelve months prior, so it can always be said, "this time last year...".

As October approached I became very apprehensive about how I (we) would feel.

Although there was the distraction of the adoption process, by late summer 2002 the meetings had become less and less. By the end of September, they had concluded.

We agreed we wanted to get away so David and I booked the first week of October off work and escaped to Solva once more.

Initially we had planned to go alone but on their suggestion, Mark and Camilla came with us and we were grateful as their presence stopped us from becoming morbid and withdrawn.

We drove down on the Friday and soon felt as though work and home were a million miles away, each day was to be filled with coastal walks and pints down the pub.

In my head I was very conscious that the forthcoming Thursday and Friday ($3^{rd}/4^{th}$) would be very emotional; however, when I woke on the Sunday before I found it hard to be enthusiastic about a planned trip to the beach.

For some reason I felt very low that day and as the others went off surfing, I took myself off to nearby St David's and soon found myself walking around the cathedral.

Anyone who has had the good fortune to visit St David's will know only too well the beautiful setting that the cathedral resides in and the emotion that can be felt when you first see it.

From the high street you do not notice the cathedral as it is nestled at the base of a steep hill. Only the tip of the clock tower alerts you to its presence.

Making your way down the cobbled lane, lined either side with picturesque, stone cottages, you still cannot comprehend what awaits you through the archway that heralds your arrival at the top of the hill.

As the building comes into view you wonder how a small town can harbour such an awesome structure; like a phoenix from the ashes, it seems to rise up from the ground in front of your very eyes.

And it doesn't matter how many times you return as you continue to remain in awe of the panoramic scene.

With my emotions running high I began to explore the vast interior, and even though I had been many times before, it is fair to say that I was "drifting" from one alcove to the next not really registering what I was seeing, nor giving any thought as to what I was doing there.

In a quiet corner was a statue of Mary with Jesus in her arms. In front were a number if chairs; about twenty or so, set in neat rows of five.

I cannot tell you why I did but I stopped and sat in the very front and just began staring at their stone faces.

Then I cried until my throat and chest ached. People passed behind; if they noticed me they didn't make it known and I didn't care if they did.

All I remember is that in my head I was asking why this had happened; nothing else.

Eventually, when the tears dried up, I returned to the beach and never spoke of it to anyone; until now (I didn't even tell David.)

We knew that we would both be dealing with our feelings in our own way (whatever that way was). For me that was the most emotional day.

From memory I think we both coped with the actual day (the 3rd) quite well but I cannot recall what we did. But I distinctly remember that on the evening of the 4th, we were playing pool in a local pub (not where I expected to be to be honest with you!)

All night I made a point of paying close attention to the clock on the wall and as 9:20pm approached, I blocked out all the noise and laughter and thought about our son. It was quite a surreal moment and I was not actually sure what I was supposed to feel.

I looked over at David who seemed oblivious to the time until I pointed it out to him. I knew from his expression that he didn't want to talk as he screwed up his face and muttered something about going to the bar.

I was initially hurt by his re-buff; however

he was soon forgiven when he later admitted to me that he had struggled with the entire day and not just that point in time. Flashbacks of walking onto the labour ward had flickered through his mind and he had found it hard to block out the scenes of my struggle to deliver Joseph, knowing that I was emotionally defeated.

He told me how the memory of seeing my little blue hospital bag packed ready and waiting by the bedroom door had extinguished the breath from his lungs.

He had hidden his anguish because he didn't want to upset me. Knowing David as I do, to admit to these emotions is very hard.

Each anniversary differs from the next. Since becoming a family the day has become easier to bare. For the first few years I would book the 4th off work, as well as the 3rd, but now I focus purely on the 3rd.

For my parents it is difficult, as it will always be their wedding anniversary. When they approached 40 years, they chose not to celebrate with one of our traditional parties. Even if they had I'm not sure if David and I would have gone.

To want to feel happiness and celebrate a day that is also tinged with sadness is very hard. I can only liken it to those who have lost loved ones on Christmas Day (for example).

Instead my parents were at my brother's and we visited them the following weekend. I will of course always send a card; that goes without saying.

21

Family, Friends and People in General

With family it is hard to talk about Joseph as they too are experiencing their own pain. For me it has changed my relationship with them. I have become hardened in my personality as I am conscious that to display too much emotion (about anything, not just Joseph) may open the floodgates that I have managed to keep locked for so long – it's a self preservation "thing".

I am someone who believes that to expose your heart in this way is a form of weakness; and I am not a weak person.

Even writing this book has been difficult and for the first time my Mum (if she chooses to read it) will find out things that I have never before discussed with her and I probably will not want to discuss even now. They remain taboo subjects.

As for David, he never talks about it. If I try to raise the subject I can see his whole body language change from relaxed to ridged; and his face will grimace at me as a sign that I am to stop.

His parents too never discuss it. Some years ago a piece was written about us in our local paper – I was angry at the proposed changes aimed to transform the hospital into a midwife only facility and felt compelled to speak out.

Did the idiots in charge not realise that in just a few minutes an apparent "routine" labour can go horribly wrong? Their argument that a doctor led labour ward was only fifteen minutes away by ambulance did not wash with me as I had barely made the operating theatre down the corridor!

Anyway, off my soap box; the point is that I had to warn Mike and Wendy about the article. I don't know if they ever read it, they certainly have never spoken about it.

Each day remains a battle. I don't care what anyone says, you can't forget when everyday things remind you of what you have lost and what you can never have back.

But you can face your demons without them getting the better of you if you stay strong.

For 98% of the time it will work, and for the other 2%? You have to have some release or else you end up bitter and twisted and resentful of other people's happiness.

Since 2004, I and three close friends (Sarah, Maria and Louise) spend a weekend away at a spa hotel, leaving the running of the house to the husbands(!); and one particular year, Sarah happened to be pregnant.

Late into the evening, as we all relaxed, the conversation turned to pregnancy and we began to relay some of our own experiences.

I too contributed, being mindful of what I said; but it was not long before a sudden wave of sadness hit me and I escaped to the toilet where I cried for a brief while before returning.

And that's what's I mean... it's hard when you have a need to feel normal and want to include yourself in such conversations; but your heart is struggling with your desire to try and talk positively about something that for you, ended in tragedy.

Even when she had her baby I wasn't one of the first to visit. I was of course ecstatic that he had arrived safe and sound as well as being pleased for her and Rod; but I was also sad for our loss.

As I have said before – I try to avoid new born babies. Some years ago I was criticised by an ex-colleague for not showing an interest in her new baby. My crime was that I was not among the others who cooed and gurgled over her son when she brought him to the office.

She paid no attention to the support and advice I had offered during her pregnancy; although internally I was in turmoil.

So when we met up months later at the staff Christmas party she was quite vocal in her opinion that we all experience tough times and I should accept that I'm not the only one who has "suffered" (her labour had proved difficult and resulted in an emergency caesarean); she even went as far as to compare my experience to another colleague who's own labour had also been traumatic.

Naturally I was very upset by this. I wasn't trying to outdo anyone or project myself as a martyr because my son had died, but I would have liked a little more understanding, considering that in both cases their children had survived.

*

But many positives have come from our loss and the impact it has had on others.

During the time I spent on adoption leave, I began working with the bereavement councillors at the hospital; every six months I would attend midwifery training days that dealt specifically with stillbirth.

By sharing my experience, it drove home to them how midwives can make the difference between a negative and positive recovery for the families involved.

I could do this because of the love and support we had received when I was in hospital.

I was also able to give advice on matters such as encouraging grieving parents to spend as much time with their child as possible and take lots of photos; it's the only chance you get.

I also stressed how important it is for a mother to hold her baby – even if at first they hold back from doing so. I so dearly wished that someone had been just that little bit more forceful with me.

The point I was trying to make was that at the time, you are not thinking logically as emotions are running high, so parents need a third person to help guide them.

My driving force to do this work was the thought that if just one couple who had lost a baby could benefit from our experience, then this gave some meaning to Joseph's death.

22

Dealing with Emotion

I have touched on many examples where emotions have played an enormous part in the past eight years; and I am certainly not naïve enough to think that they won't continue to do so.

As part of my self-preservation policy, I have learnt to control them – at least 98% of the time; and at the expense of my relationship with others.

To speak about our experience means switching off my emotions and focusing only on the facts in a calm and precise manner - ask me anything about what happened and I will tell you; but ask me about how I felt and you won't necessarily get a response.

This book has allowed me to bring that side of things out into the open; it's easier to write than talk.

Six months following Joseph's death, I began counselling. When I was in hospital all we needed (wanted) were family and friends, but now I needed to talk the "problem" through with someone who was emotionally detached from us.

I didn't know what to expect or even where to begin, so I think we started with how I was coping at that point in time; and eventually we moved onto the actual event itself.

It was agreed that in order to move forward, I needed to have the blanks filled in and this meant knowing what had transpired during the operation itself.

To obtain this information I would be allowed access to my medical file and, for the first time since my discharge, I would meet with Delyth Rich. (David, you will have noticed, was not involved in any of the meetings I had, but was fully supportive of my decision to go. I didn't think any less of him for not accompanying me. He was dealing with our loss in his own way and I had to respect that; even if I still think he should talk about it more!)

To meet Delyth was a turning point in my understanding of the enormity of my illness. Up until that point I still could not comprehend how close to death I had been.

As she approached me in the corridor I was suddenly aware of how petite she was. It's bizarre the things that go through your mind! This was the woman who had delivered our son and had had the privilege of holding him; she was (is) among the few individuals whereby an invisible bond has been forged that will never be broken.

In a soft voice she began telling me everything and I sat in silence; I was like a sponge absorbing what she said.

She spoke of how she wasn't even supposed to be on duty that night and at the last minute, switched shifts with another colleague.

How she had realised something was wrong when stitching me following Joseph's birth; something to do with the lack of blood present at the cut; this had prompted her to ask for my pulse to be checked (this was not a routine procedure and at first it was thought that the machine was malfunctioning because Clare couldn't get a reading, but it quickly became apparent that I was the problem, not the machine).

Delyth firmly believed that had I not had an episiotomy, I would be dead – those few moments required for her to remain in the room with David and I, had meant my haemorrhage was realised in time. It was also fundamental in relation to how quickly the crash team were called and able to deal with the emergency (following on from that night, Delyth called for a review of procedures within the department and safe guards were put in place including the implementation of routine observations).

Once the seriousness of my condition had been established and I was transferred to theatre, Delyth was part of the team who worked tirelessly to repair the bleed.

She detailed how my organs were failing in an attempt to preserve the brain; she spoke of collapsing veins, blood loss (hence the 46 units) and how, amongst all the trauma, she had to face David. It was Delyth that told me David had collapsed to his knees when I was in ICU and it was thought I had begun to bleed again. She was also the one who described the moment I awoke and how everyone started crying. And she also shared with me an instance when the operation was complete and as I lay next door in theatre waiting to be transferred, the whole team took stock of what had happened over a cup of tea!

This made me smile; it was light relief after everything I had been told.

Understandably when it was time to leave, I felt numb.

I have not seen nor spoken to Delyth since that day. She transferred to another hospital but I understand that the whole event left a lasting impression on her.

However, years later I was reading a magazine, local to the area; I turned a page and there she was, running an advice column with Mr Beattie on pregnancy and childbirth. It was a weird moment for me as found myself suddenly looking at the woman who had saved my life.

It was also around this time that not being able to have children began to sink in.

I felt useless and although we had begun the adoption process, nothing can ever replace the feeling of failure that comes from the fact that you cannot bare your own child.

David always reassured me that it didn't matter, he was pleased to have me alive; but my head would not let it go and it became a contributing factor to the deep depression that would set in from time to time.

Periods in my life when the grief was over whelming, I would wake in the night and it would hit me like a train.

Without waking David I would escape to downstairs and cry uncontrollably; real sobs that came from deep within. It was so bad that I had to physically lie down as every part of my body felt drained.

Then, when the grief had passed, I would return to bed and make excuses as to why my eyes were all puffed up in the morning.

David was not aware this was happening. I wanted to protect him from any more worry so I kept it secret for four years. I did however share it with the councillors as I needed to offload on someone.

Their suggestion was to go back to see Mr Roberts as I may now be suffering from the early stages of a menopause (sometimes triggered by a hysterectomy); but I had naturally assumed that it was my system trying to relieve the pain, it had never crossed my mind that it could be a hormonal imbalance.

In 2005, under the watchful and caring eye of Mr Roberts, I began my treatment. For six months I was given injections to stop my ovaries working to see if I was better without them.

Within a month the change in me was incredible, and visibly noticeable. I felt alive again. It was a feeling of having emerged from a dense fog. The conclusion was obvious, so in 2006 the remainder of my female organs were removed.

(Do I feel any less feminine? No. In fact I feel liberated).

The operation brought back many memories (Mr Roberts did warn me of this). However I was fortunate enough to go private so David did not have to return to the same hospital or visit me on my old ward; but it was evident that he felt very uncomfortable being back in a medical environment.

As for me; although the procedure would be more controlled, I was still very apprehensive about being put to sleep and became emotional whilst the team prepped me for theatre.

But within days I was home, albeit a bit sore. Encouraged by me, David escaped to his brothers for a few days shortly after my return home because I could tell it was hurting him to see me so uncomfortable once more; a move that was criticised by my family.

But I had wanted him to go as we each needed to recover both physically and mentally.

Our son stayed with Mike and Wendy so there wasn't an issue regarding childcare; and for me it meant that I could have the bed to myself!

I still have moments when my emotions take me by surprise but these are triggered more by TV or music, or the loss of someone I have known.

When a colleague in work died suddenly, the whole company attended his funeral. He was a lovely man with a young family. As the service progressed I found that I was awash with emotion when the minister referred to the pain his mother was feeling at her loss; he said "no mother should ever have to bury her son" - those words hit me hard.

I struggle when I hear "Adagio for Strings". It was played when they brought my Gran's coffin into the chapel. It reminds me not only of her, but also of being pregnant.

September 11th 2001 holds its own memories for me. Like most people, I can remember exactly what I was doing the day it happened: I had begun working on my music tape for my impending labour when a friend called and asked if I was watching the news.

Much later, in 2007, I visited Ground Zero whilst in New York on business. There was a book signing being held in the church where the firemen had rested. The official photographer was there, promoting his book (all proceeds to charity).

My dad had been a London Fire Fighter, so I knew he would appreciate a copy; as I spoke with the author about that day I became very emotional. I apologised and explained that I was pregnant at the time and had lost my son. He was very kind and expressed his sympathy for me; I felt foolish.

Also in 2001 I appeared on Ready Steady Cook when I was six months pregnant. The show was aired one month following Joseph's funeral.

I watched it. But it felt somewhat ironic that when asked by Ainsley if I wanted a boy or a girl, I had replied I didn't care as long as it was healthy.

David didn't watch it. Never has.

In 2004 we wanted to move house. Mike and Wendy also had theirs on the market and as it had a huge garden and we a young child, we decided theirs would be an ideal choice.

Although neither of us spoke about it at the time, we both knew that buying this house would mean passing the cemetery and Joseph every single day. It did not concern me but I worried about David. However he was the main instigator in buying his parents place so I knew he was ok about it.

From our bedroom window you can see the arch and the old Sunday School; I know that just behind lies our son. It's a great comfort to know that we have him close to us.

*

And there are times when events that have happened in other peoples' lives (although tragic) bring relief as I can associate my hurt with theirs and gain strength from them.

I remember in particular a programme presented by Michael Portillo about a childhood friend who had committed suicide.

Although the circumstances differed, I could relate to much of what his parents said about their son. They spoke of not being able to say his name; for years we referred to Joseph as "the baby". It's still difficult even now to say his name out loud.

Also the immense sadness of wondering what their son would have been like, what choices would he have made in life.

Their pain was still evident in their faces even after many years; but they have managed to get through life together; so will we.

23

What Now?

David and I will be ten years married this year (well in about a week actually)... for eight of those years we have had to live with what has happened.

Has it changed us? Yes of course is has, what you have to ask is has it changed our relationship for the better? People change as they get older and marriages develop; you become more (or less!) tolerant of each others' habits and in time, as you settle into it, you realise that what binds you together is the realisation that you just can't imagine life without your partner.

I do wonder what we would have been like if our marriage had been allowed to mature gradually. With so much to contend with, inevitably cracks have appeared from time to time. There have been arguments, accusations, lack of understanding (on both parts), frustration, anger, sadness and tears.

But we seem always to be able to glue the cracks back together and get on with things; and we can still laugh together. What the future will be like I don't know. I wonder what surprises my body will continue to throw at me (aged 36 I began taking HRT, needless to say I try not to pay any attention to the press regarding links to breast cancer and trust in the advice of my doctors).

I have scars that are physical as well as mental. I hate them, but for David they are a positive remainder of how fortunate he is to still have me with him.

I wonder too who will look after Joseph when we are dead and buried? So many unattended graves are scattered around the cemetery; will his eventually be one? Will people walk by and comment? Will they even notice him?

David and I will remain proud parents to two beautiful boys. We shall always carry this chapter of our lives with us. Each October we will comment as to how old Joseph would have been. Asking the same question, what would he have been like?

We've stopped wishing it had never happened because then we wouldn't have Jake; we are torn between wanting to be with both but knowing that to have one is to be without the other.

People are always saying that time is a great healer. I don't think that's true. I think that what time does is allow you to get use to whatever it is you're trying to overcome; find a way to live with it. The hurt never goes; you simply have to learn to numb it out, well most of the time. Time cannot change that we still had a son; and he died.

But let's be happy!

Happy that there is a little boy who has a wonderful life with a family that love him dearly; whose spoilt for all the right reasons; who has a brother who lives in heaven.

He knows that he too is special because we chose him and wouldn't swap him for the world.

Someone said that he was the little boy who won the lottery.
I think it was us that had the winning ticket.